BEYOND PETULANCE:

Republican Politics and the Future of America

BEYOND PETULANCE:

Republican Politics and the Future of America

DR. RAULSTON B. NEMBHARD

Published by:
Olde Wharf Publishers
8413 Clematis Lane
Orlando, Florida 32819

www.OldMountainPress.com

Copyright © 2014 Dr. Raulston B. Nembhard
Cover Design by Jason Jones,
Studio Jones Design-www.studiojonesdesign.com
Interior text design by Tom Davis
ISBN: 0-9713049-4-7

First Edition
Printed and bound in the United States of America
1 2 3 4 5 6 7 8 9 10

Dedicated to all the Apostles of social justice who struggle for fairness and equity for their fellow human beings.

ACKNOWLEDGMENT

I am grateful to a number of people who have given me the opportunity to discuss and critique with them many of the topics in this book. Their willingness to engage me has sharpened my understanding of the dangers and opportunities confronting America and of the hopeful and viable future that can be built for all its citizens.

My gratitude is extended to Tom Davis and his staff at Old Mountain Press for their work in formatting and typesetting the script in readiness for publication. Finally, to my wife, Heather, who has been patient, amidst her myriad activities, to painstakingly read the manuscript, offer valuable advice and correcting the proofs. Her insights and suggestions have kept me encouraged and on an even course.

CONTENTS

INTRODUCTION 1

CHAPTER ONE 7
OF ICED TEA AND FROZEN CAKES: The Battle for the Heart
and Soul of the Republican Party.

CHAPTER TWO 35
THE IMMIGRATION IMPERATIVE

CHAPTER THREE 57
THE IMPERATIVE OF SOCIAL JUSTICE

CHAPTER FOUR 91
REBUILDING THE ERODED FOUNDATIONS

CHAPTER FIVE 123
THE SHINING CITY ON A HILL

INTRODUCTION

The prolonged economic crisis has severely tested the will and resilience of the American people. Nowhere is this more evident than in the high unemployment rate, the crisis in the housing industry with unprecedented foreclosures brought on by the meltdown on Wall Street, the moral confusion about our identity as a nation, the threatened decimation of the middle class and a host of other problems that confront the country.

It would not be fair or true to assert that any one political party or group can be held responsible for the dysfunctional politics that we see in Washington and in many of our state legislatures. The far right of the political spectrum will assert that the problems are a manifestation of the Democratic Party's incompetence. More specifically, that it is a result of the presidency of Barack Obama who, in the estimation of some, has brought an amateurish approach to governance in the White House.

The far left or left of center will blame the recalcitrant Republicans and certainly the eight years of fiscal irresponsibility under the George W Bush administration. This blame-game tends to trivialize the perils that face the country and diverts attention from what needs to be done to fix the problems. The level of petty politics on both sides of the political divide is disgusting and is hurting the country in very significant ways.

The Standards and Poor downgrade of the nation's credit rating in 2011 was a sad result of this politics of obstruction and petulance. We have lurched from one manufactured and self-inflicted crisis to the next. In a grand display of political *harakiri*, we have inflicted unnecessary wounds on the nation's body politic in order to sustain narrow partisan ideological positions. Polling data show that an increasing number of Americans have become disillusioned with the political process. They have either withdrawn from it completely, or have simply become

1

resigned to a futility that they cannot do anything to effect change for the better.

A significant characteristic of this frustration is the anti-establishment paranoia that has gripped certain sections of the population and which has seen a dramatic increase in hate groups that have armed themselves in preparation for the ultimate political Armageddon. Cynicism about America's future has become almost pernicious and might be at its worse since the Vietnam Era. This cynicism and disenchantment with the political process has placed the country's democratic way of life under great threat. At no time has the notion of America as an exceptional nation been more severely tested; and at no time has the urgency for an informed and engaged citizenry become more palpable and relevant.

While acknowledging that no one group or party can be blamed for the problems that America faces, disturbing trends have emerged in Republican politics in recent times which should be cause for great concern to those who regard America as an exceptional nation. These trends are worrying as they go to the heart of the viability of the nation's democratic way of life as the Founding Fathers so eloquently understood it. It can be reasonably questioned whether the Republican Party as presently constituted is the party of Lincoln, Eisenhower, or even Reagan, Jack Kemp or Bob Dole. As it now stands it is a party unworthy of its proud history. A shadow of its former self, it has disintegrated into disparate factions without any core philosophy to define and guide a viable pathway to progress.

There is no doubt that a gigantic battle is being waged for the heart and soul of the party. But there is a palpable paralysis of leadership on the part of those who should be leading the charge or at least demonstrating the courage necessary to reassert the historical elements that once made the party respectable. Instead, one sees the absence of core convictions as is evidenced by a willingness to pander to interest groups in defense of ideology which often runs counter to the public good. This puts the country's honor at risk and in the process hurts whatever reputation it has as an exceptional nation.

America's reputation as a caring and gentle nation which takes care of its own and the stranger among in its midst has been sullied in recent times. From the war in Iraq to its ambivalent approach to comprehensive immigration reform, to its abysmal record in treating with women's issues, the Republican Party has found itself in opposition to issues that an increasing number of Americans care deeply about. This has led to much questioning of the party's sincerity about a secure and vibrant future for America. Deep, philosophical reflection on the intractable problems that the nation faces seems to elude them. Such reflection is often replaced by facile, superficial commentary that hardly does any justice to the presenting problems of the day.

Why should any American be concerned about the viability of the Republican Party? As an integral part of the political infrastructure of the country, the simple answer is that for good or ill the country needs the Republican Party, but it needs a party that can demonstrate the openness and bipartisan compromise that will make government function in the best interests of the people. The reason for the rising frustration of citizens with the political process in Washington is precisely because they do not feel that their government is acting in their best interests. For many, there is not a great deal that they can feel good about. What with rising unemployment and the inability of people to access health care and even keep their homes? What with the continued escalation in the poverty rate and the widening gap between the richest one percent and the 99 percent? What of the almost 17 trillion dollars debt load which has made the nation for all intents and purposes, bankrupt?

Yet, in the midst of these and other troubles, they see a party at war with itself and which has taken the art of non-compromise to a new level. Worst, they see a party that is fast elevating petulance to an organizing principle of political action. This is not only reflected in the rigid adherence of many of that party's members to certain orthodoxies, such as no tax increases, but in mindless obstruction of the policies of the president, even if these policies can redound to the good of the country.

In recent times this political temper tantrum has become too much a distressing feature of the resume of too many Republicans in Congress. It is galling to onlookers, many of whom are constituents of these Congress persons, to see this petulant display. It is especially galling when it is done in the Senate given the high esteem in which this body ought to be held. Yet, the many Republican filibusters that have rendered that body almost impotent in recent times might be the greatest display of the petulance that has come to define legislators in Washington.

A single-minded commitment to peeve on the part of policymakers, of whatever stripe, debilitates the reputation of the legislature and in time becomes a corrupting influence which undermines the very foundations of the country's democratic way of life. In the process debate is coarsened and positions hardened between both sides of the political divide. In the end critical decisions on matters of national importance are hindered or stymied.

The essential danger and logical outcome of Republican petulance is the further alienation of that party from the electorate which may very well set the stage for the dictatorship of one party. People do not expect the parties to agree all the time but they do expect them to govern with a spirit of compromise and forbearance. There can be hard, long and even fierce discussion of various viewpoints but Americans have come to expect that in the end their elected leaders will do what is best for them by setting aside their own political ambitions and prejudices and do what is good for the country.

Whether they want to acknowledge it or not, many have placed the Republican Party at the center of the collective depression that has settled on so many in the nation. This cannot be good for a political party that hopes to lead the government in the future. There is a great deal of work to be done and the party is challenged to reclaim its proud legacy, to redefine itself and to be the party that the people can once more become comfortable with to trust with presidential power. The party is presently adrift on a sea of moral confusion but the palpable truth is that America needs the Republican Party to be strong and healthy. But it must be mindful of the things that ail it and seek to heal them.

In critiquing the Republican Party in this book, the immediate charge will be that I am being partisan or biased in my views. It is not easy to dissuade persons from this position, but it may help to know that at present I am by registration, political instinct and persuasion an

Independent. My interest lies in what redounds to the greater good of the country and I will stand side by side in support of anyone and any party that eschews cronyism, skullduggery and malfeasance in pursuing the country's interest. An exceptional nation needs a robust democracy in which all views can contend and be respected for the greater good of the country.

The Republican Party is in the spotlight precisely because it is fast losing that sense of its place in building this robust democracy. It is fast becoming a fringe party. Its self-marginalization is making it a mere outpost in the American political landscape and this is not good for the long term health of the nation. We must remain optimistic that things will change for the better, but we cannot be blinkered to the existential threat that perpetual political rigidity and gridlock pose to the nation. The party can and must do better so it can prove itself worthy of the proud history it once enjoyed.

....

Raulston B. Nembhard
Orlando, Florida
February, 2014

CHAPTER ONE

OF ICED TEA AND FROZEN CAKES: The Battle for the Heart and Soul of the Republican Party.

With malice toward none, with charity for all, with firmness in the right as God gives us to see the right, let us strive on to finish the work we are in, to bind up the nation's wounds, to care for him who shall have borne the battle and for his widow and his orphan, to do all which may achieve and cherish a just and lasting peace among ourselves and with all nations.—-
(Abraham Lincoln- Second Inaugural Address, March 4,1865).

<<<<<<>>>>>>

The defeat of the Republican Party in the last presidential elections confirmed what many people already knew: the party is broken and in need of urgent repair and restoration. In a candid and scathing critique of the party on *Fox News Sunday*,[1] former Republican presidential candidate, Bob Dole, who in his days in the senate was known to be a moderate on conservative issues, said that neither himself nor the iconic president Reagan could make it in the Republican Party as presently constituted. He recommended that the party should hang a sign which read "closed for repairs" on the doors until they can come up with some positive ideas. It is not only Bob Dole who has become exasperated with what the party is becoming. Louisiana Governor, Bobby Jindal, characterized the party as the party of the "stupid." In an op-ed in *Politico*, he urged the Republican leadership to "stop the bedwetting" and put on "their big-boy pants."[2] For people who believe in good governance, it is painful to see what the party has become: a

7

squabbling, decadent entity that is out of touch with the needs and aspirations of the American people. There is no doubt that it desperately needs transformational leadership that can lead it to a place of respectability. What the last election made clear is the absence of the kind of bold leadership that is required to reconfigure the party into a cohesive and respectable entity that the people can once more trust with power. The party is clearly fractured yet there is not a unifying philosophy that can engage a sober conversation as to the way forward.

The clearest voices of reason are drowned out by the loud decibels of a petulant and vocal minority. Individuals like Governor Christie of New Jersey who speak up about the need for change, are either vilified, marginalized or dismissed as not possessing the requisite conservative credentials. They are not invited to important conservative confabs such as the 2012 CPAC convention which prominently excluded Christie. His embrace of Obama in the aftermath of the devastation of sections of his state by hurricane Sandy was enough to make his conservative credentials suspect.

The Romney Factor

With regard to Romney, one would have thought that having just carried the banner of the party into a presidential election he would have been best suited to provide some direction to the party, even in defeat. But no one within or outside the party is hopeful that this will happen anytime soon or that it will ever happen. The few comments he has made since the election have been quite superficial and trite and do not amount to what a frazzled party requires to establish

> *The clearest voices of reason are drowned out by the loud decibels of a petulant and vocal minority.*

credibility with the public. From the beginning, Romney's conservative credentials were suspect. He was never really welcomed by the militant

8

right wing of the party. They threw their lot in with him only because he rose to the top of the pile that sought the party's presidential nomination. And what a pile it was.

Having gotten there he did not carve out an overarching philosophy of what he wanted to do and where he would take the country as a conservative Republican president. He waffled and wavered and at times was not truthful about what he really believed. At times he came across as a bottle into which anything that was poured would fit. He pandered to whatever group in the party he believed had to be relied upon to give him victory. In doing this he came across as confused to the voter and as heartless as when he pronounced on some positions such as his love for poor people, his "47 percent" comments and his ability to fire people. His problems were exacerbated by his Democratic opponents defining him from very early as a rabid capitalist who would be an enemy of the middle class.

It is not farfetched to suggest that as the party searches for new leadership, Mr. Romney will become a mere footnote to the party as President G.W.Bush became in the 2012 campaign. It may also be that even if Romney had won the presidency he might have gone on to be a poor leader of the Republican Party. It is doubtful that he could have provided the kind of forceful thinking that would have been required to move the country into a decisively new direction. Far from being seen as a voice of reason and respectability, he seems destined to be consigned to a mere fundraising role in the party. He did not only conduct a poorly run election but one that did not have the gravitas and credibility to win crucial constituents necessary for victory. However, although he has to bear a great deal of the blame for the election loss, it is unfair to hold him responsible for the many afflictions from which the party suffers. His positions on the many issues that were rejected by the electorate were symptomatic of a party in decline and a party which was out of touch, and still is, with a changing America.

A Party in Decline

The sad truth is that the brand of the Republican Party has been severely damaged and a great deal of work has got to be done for voters to become comfortable to entrust it with presidential power in the future. They have to undertake the painstaking and difficult task that credible soul-searching requires and which acknowledges the damage to its brand and what will be required to repair it in order to return it to a path of viability. So far, utterances from party spokespersons and legislative behavior in the Congress and states controlled by Republican majorities, give little satisfaction that the Republicans have learned their lessons from the last election. If anything, they seem to be doubling down on the stupidity that Jindal assailed especially with respect to women's reproductive rights and their general attitude to women's issues. One would have thought that on sober reflection even they would have found their approach to women in the run up to the elections objectionable and reprehensible. But this has not been the case.

Since the elections, more time has been wasted pushing anti-women issues and trying to repeal the Affordable Care Act, (derisively labeled Obamacare by its detractors), than has been spent dealing with the real issues of jobs and building a sound economy that people really care about.

For at least the last four years, the Republican Party has placed itself on the wrong side of issues that worry Americans when they go to bed at nights. By legislative action and plain vitriolic rhetoric, they have proven themselves unequal to the task on such issues as education for our young, healthcare reform, women's rights, gender equality at the workplace and the rights of ethnic minorities in a multicultural, diverse and pluralistic society. By their own incendiary rhetoric they have communicated a message that they really do not care and by doing so they have simply alienated a large chunk of the electorate. This has not been helped by their comfortable relationship with the rich, powerful interest groups to whom they are indebted and who pull their ideological strings. Their perceived lack of concern for the poor and marginalized has alienated them from an already beaten up middle-class.

A Racist Party?

The not too subtle racist comments by leading spokespersons of the party have reinforced the narrative that the party is racist or generally unwelcoming to minorities. Members of the party would like to claim that they do not support racism, but in the words of Colonel Lawrence Wilkerson, former Chief of Staff of General Colin Powell, the party contains a lot of racists.[3] Even General Powell's endorsement of President Obama was seen by surrogates of the Romney campaign as influenced by both men being of the same ethnic stripe.

There has never been another presidential election in recent memory in which there have been more coded messages of racism sent than this. In fact, the racial tone of the 2012 campaign was more evident than in 2008. In some instances, racist remarks were less than covert whether in advertisements or spoken by important spokespersons of the party. Some of these spokespersons seemed to have found it difficult to even bring themselves to say "President Obama" or ""Mr. Obama." It was either "Barack" as if they were friends of his, or "Obama" in order to diminish his status. The demeaning caricatures of the president during the formation of the Tea Party were among the grossest attempts to delegitimize and belittle the president. He was accused of being a socialist and of wanting to turn America into a European-style socialist country. In the thinking of those who should know better, such as John Sununu, former governor of New Hampshire, the President was lazy and incompetent.[4] The purveyors of the "birther" movement lie in the same race baiting trajectory as do those who question the president's legitimacy as an American citizen and his contrived Mau, Mau antecedents.

It is one thing to make unwarranted and bigoted statements in the heat of an election campaign, but quite another when these things are seen to be an integral part of your belief system or that of the organization to which you belong. The precise problem which confronts the Republican Party is the perception of many that the party is racist and that it operates as an exclusive white club where minorities are not welcomed. One only had to look at images out of the last Republican Convention in Tampa to get a good idea of where the party was and still is in terms of cultural diversity and appeal to minorities. The party can live in denial if it so chooses, but it is certainly not a "big tent" party that can attract big ideas and endear people to it readily. This is a reality about which it will have to have an honest conversation as the battle for its heart and soul intensifies.

A Changing America: Two Visions, Two Pathways

Another reality that the election results should have brought home forcibly to the Republicans is that America is changing. Stubborn refusal to recognize the changing demographics in the country will lend impetus to the continued decline of the party. Sections of the conservative press represented largely by the *Fox News Network*, were alarmed at how much the country has changed. Bill O'Reilly, one of the network's important purveyors, almost ashen-faced, told a Fox News program that the white Establishment is now the minority; that the demographics are changing and that we do not have traditional America anymore. [5] What he meant by a traditional America was not clearly articulated, but he was right that the country is changing. His critique that the change is represented in America becoming a socially progressive entitlement society or a nanny state misses the point entirely. The changing dynamics are captured in two visions, two pathways for America that were presented in the campaign and portrayed on the platforms of both parties at their national conventions. These two visions underscore that America is still a divided nation; that it is indeed in the grip of an identity crisis. By way of poetic justice for Mr. Romney, 47 percent of America in the elections subscribed to his vision of an unbridled capitalism unimpeded by any restriction from government. At the heart of this vision is a ruthless selfishness that

12

unbridled individual freedom is at the heart of any drive to succeed. This is the essence of Ayn Rand philosophy which Mr. Ryan was forced to awkwardly disavow. By this philosophy the government owed you nothing; you are on your own.

The other vision of a more inclusive, progressive society was best explained by the "Explainer in Chief", Bill Clinton, in a way that neither Romney, Ryan nor even Obama could have done. Speaking at the Democratic Convention he gave clarity to what these two paths were about.

> *My fellow Americans you have to decide what kind of country you want to live in. If you want a you're-on-your-own, winner-take-all, you should support the Republican ticket. If you want a country of shared responsibilities-we're-all-in-this together society-you should vote for Barack Obama and Joe Biden.[6]*

On November 6, 53 percent of the electorate decided that they want a country of shared responsibilities where everyone played by the rules and where government can become a true facilitator of people's progress instead of being a hindrance. They voted for an America defined by mutual survival, interdependence, tolerance and yes, compromise for the good of society. They rejected the social Darwinism of 19th-century society which emphasized ruthless competition where the fittest survive at the expense of the weak and marginalized; a system governed by raw, predatory, unbridled capitalism in which its actors do not believe that the rules apply to them. The voters rejected an unfettered capitalism for one that is subject to some form of regulation because they had seen the devastating and ruinous effects of what the rich can do when the government is not watching as it ought. Capitalism free of state regulation is not what the new American character is about. It is not what makes for an exceptional nation.

In voting for a caring, sharing and more responsible society the voters made the point that their interests are best served when things are spread equitably in the society, not when a few are able to live high off its largesse to the detriment of its weaker and poorer members. The Republicans, and especially the Tea Party, hate "big government" for precisely the reason that government often has to be the shield that protects the vulnerable from the talons of the rich and powerful. The election results should concretize in our minds that America has entered a post Ayn Rand society where unselfish contribution to society for its greater good is at a premium.

The conservative right is in a panic mode precisely because they continue to misread the message sent by the electorate. This may explain why the lament of the demise of the white establishment is so loud and why the nostalgia for traditional America is so palpable. It cannot be taken for granted that a more interdependent and mutually inclusive society will be realized anytime soon. There is still a lot of tension between the two visions or pathways for America's future. The election results might have subdued it for the moment, but if the fiscal cliff debacle and the recent debate on keeping the government open and raising the debt limit are anything to go by, no one should entertain the illusion that the vision to maintain a rabid capitalist America has died. America has already been awakened to the disturbing signs that there are those in the Republican Party who are prepared to return to their petulant ways in shutting down the federal government if they cannot have their way in scrapping, for example, the Affordable Care Act. There should be no illusions that what special interest groups failed to win openly through the polls they will seek to gain by stealth. They may operate below the radar, but they are no less committed to having their way. For some, "payback" has not died because the Democrats won the election. A lot of money was spent by rich supporters of the GOP through the Super PACs and it would be naïve to think that having lost an election they will simply disappear. You can expect them to be very active on Capitol Hill as they seek to influence politicians to give them "stuff" to which they feel themselves entitled.

In fact, because of the election results, the plutocrats are likely to strengthen their hegemonic grip on the GOP. One wonders whether we have not begun to see this in the stubbornness that is coming from the GOP members in the House. It is clear that these members have their eyes set on future financial support from their big donors and will do everything in their power to give succor to their unenlightened self interests. Their petulant obduracy is no doubt aimed at pleasing the base of the party for which they are obviously contemptuous. Republican petulance is a function of big monied interests being pleased with the shenanigans of Republican politicians in Congress. What we are witnessing as dysfunctional politics in Washington is no more than the unholy alliance between petulant politics and big money. Until the president understands the nexus between big money and Republican petulance he will never be able to appreciate the mountain he has to climb to get anything done.

> *Until the president understands the nexus between big money and Republican petulance, he will never be able to appreciate the mountain he has to climb to get anything done.*

Can the Republican Party Recover?

Americans are right to be worried as they question the future viability of the Republican Party. While no one should be in a hurry to write its obituary, the party has suffered some serious wounds most of them self-inflicted which need to be tended. Most Americans will agree that it is imperative that the party recovers as they know that it is an essential component of the country's ongoing democratic vitality. Americans instinctively abhor dictatorship and know the danger represented by a political vacuum when a major party becomes too weak and moribund or is seen to abdicate its responsibility to the process of good governance. They know that government works best when there is compromise;

when the people they elect are prepared to huddle together and work on tough issues that will lead to sane policies for the health of the nation. America is strongest when there is a counterbalance between prevailing liberal and conservative ideals which can present people with real options. This could explain why the dysfunction of our political elites in Washington is so painful to watch

What is clear to most well-thinking Americans, both inside and outside the party, is that for any meaningful recovery to occur there has to be some fundamental change in the way the party conducts its business. It cannot be business as usual. It has to win back the confidence of core constituencies and recover the conservative philosophical ideals that once defined it as a great party. In other words, it has to recapture aspects of its historical antecedents that made it a great party and of which in its present dispensation it has become unworthy. Whatever may be the way forward, there are a number of imperatives that need to be addressed if the party is to recover and gain traction in the eyes of the American people, especially the important middle class. We will address some here.

1. Return to the pristine conservative values that once informed it.

The crisis in the Republican Party is largely a crisis of ideology. Having abandoned its premier conservative philosophical principles for abstract, hardcore ideologies, the party has become devoid of any cogent moral underpinnings. It has fast become a frustrated party in the full grips of an identity crisis. There is no leader of the stature of a Reagan and even Eisenhower that can be depended on to lead it into something that the American voter can once more trust to lead the country. Having been decoupled from its conservative moorings it is now adrift on a sea of uncertainty. This is often manifested in the bewildering cries of leading persons in the conservative movement who decry what the party is fast becoming. The problem is not that the party is not given to conservative principles -family values, small government, fiscal responsibility, strong national defense, to name a few- but in the articulation of those

16

principles in recent times, those who speak for the party come across as weird (as in legitimate rape when discussing family values) or misogynistic (when addressing abortion, contraception and other issues relating to women). Values which Republicans see as essential to conservative philosophy have merely become loud shrieks from a party that has too many disparate voices speaking for it, each seeking its own agenda and self-promotion, but all enunciating extremely dogmatic positions that a growing number of Americans find hard to accept.

So, in the present configuration of the Republican Party, it is difficult to determine what "pristine" conservative values are anymore. Almost daily, Republicans in Congress remind us of how difficult the task is for they are still demonstrating that they are the Grand Old Party of obstruction. Their failure to vote in a timely manner on relief to hurricane ravaged Americans in New York and New Jersey left even many Republicans in shock. New Jersey governor Chris Christie was very enraged at their dalliance and in his inimitable way did not mince words in expressing his outrage. Of equal repugnance was the failure of Senate Republicans to support a Bill that would guarantee integrity of treatment to disabled veterans around the world. Their recalcitrance was a slap in the face of former Senator Bob Dole, himself a disabled veteran and war hero, who came to the Senate, perhaps for the last time, to cheer on what was clearly to him and to others a done deal. One needs not mention the stated desire by Republican leaders in Congress to make the good faith and credit of the American government a hostage to political brinksmanship.

The difficulties facing the party have not been helped by problems within the conservative movement itself. There does not seem to be any consensus about what the movement stands for today. What now passes for conservatism would make that icon of modern American conservatism, William Buckley, very embarrassed. He understood the fundamental, philosophical underpinnings on which a vital conservative movement had to be structured if it were to be a successful counterbalance to the prevailing liberal ideology of the day. He spent a great deal of his life defining and refining what these philosophical positions meant and their significance in the growth of American democratic ideals.

But today the movement is under siege not necessarily from the political left or from liberal ideology in general, but from the internal meltdown of vital ideas within its own camp. Both the conservative movement in general and the Republican Party in particular are bedeviled by a polyglot of divergent views that lack the capacity to bring a coherent set of ideas around which people can coalesce. What now passes for conservatism is an assortment of radical and fanatical ideas that are tossed around by many who call themselves conservatives but whose very actions negate the legitimate values of conservatism. As a result fertile ground has been prepared for all kinds of wacky ideas to grow and flourish. We saw a number of these ideas during the November campaign. "Legitimate rape" might have been one of the wackiest, but there were others as could be seen in the kind of scorched-earth rhetoric that spewed from the microphone of leading talk show hosts such as Rush Limbaugh who has been instrumental in shaping the views of a large constituency of Republican voters. Such rhetoric has not lent any legitimacy to what pristine conservative values are about.

In a recent article in the *Weekly Standard,* William Kristol, one of the leading conservative voices, echoed concern for what he described as the decline of the conservative movement. He was critical of the parlous state in which the conservative movement finds itself. As a leading purveyor of conservative ideology, he was pained to admit that the conservative movement is in disarray. In the article he was even more caustic and scathing in his critique of where the movement now stands. He wrote:

> *Reading about some conservative organizations and Republican campaigns these days, one is reminded of Eric Hoffer's remark, "Every great cause begins as a movement, becomes a business, and eventually degenerates into a racket." It may be that major parts of American conservatism have become such a racket that a kind of*

18

refounding of the movement as a cause is necessary. A reinvigoration of the Republican party also seems desirable, based on a new generation of leaders, perhaps coming-as did Ike and Reagan-from outside the normal channels.[7]

It is not clear what he meant by the re-founding of the conservative movement and who will take responsibility for this. There is no one of the stature of a William Buckley who has the presence and fecundity of mind to do what Kristol might be suggesting. As was suggested before, if Buckley were alive he would be profoundly saddened at what the movement has become and racket does not even begin to describe it.

Whatever remains of the movement has been hijacked by hostile elements that are only concerned about their rugged, individual interests and not about the kind of patriotic thinking that once gave the movement force and relevance. Ayn Rand individualism with its recourse to vicious competitive capitalism, in which the winner takes all, has become the dominant philosophy in some sections of the movement. In Republican politics this has spawned a mean-spiritedness which has fast become a defining feature of the Republican Party. It is no surprise that what ails the conservative movement is coterminous with what ails the Republican Party.

There is no doubt that a reinvigoration of the Republican Party is desirable but who is going to lead the charge? Senator Rubio? Congressman Ryan? Governors Bobby Jindal and Chris Christie? Donald Trump? Who will have the temerity to stand up to the big money backers of the party who are only motivated by their own self interests and could not be bothered with the humbug of a pure conservative ideology? Who will have the intestinal fortitude to administer the tough medicine that is required to loosen the parasitic hold of the Tea Party and flush it from the Republican system? Who will be bold and honest enough to speak the truth about the failures of the party and realign it with the kind of conservative values that once made it proud?

These are critical questions that have to be answered by anyone who believes he or she can lead the party to greatness and viability. The person who is merely interested in winning political power as an end in itself is not the kind of person that the party needs at this time. Neither is the person who is willing to go in any direction in which the political wind blows. The party requires and deserves a leader who will challenge it to move in fundamentally new directions from the path that the plutocrats want it to be on.

2. Prove itself to be a party that is not hostile to immigration.
The Republican Party has to work the hardest in proving itself to be a welcoming party. One of the best ways in which it can demonstrate this is by working vigorously to pass comprehensive immigration reform. The matter of immigration will be given fuller treatment later in our analysis, but it is sufficient to say here that Republican rhetoric on immigration has been particularly poisonous. The party needs to win new friends but it is doing everything within its power to ensure that it remains an isolated outpost in a far flung desert of American politics. A party that shows that its expertise lies mainly in alienating people from its camp will only seek to gain political power by default or brinksmanship. The party has a chance to prove before the end of 2013 or not long thereafter, that it is serious about immigration reform. Some of the Senate Republicans have caught on, but the rhetoric from House Republicans does not give much hope that they want to be on the right side of the debate.

3. Prove that it is really committed to being an inclusive, big tent party that is aware of the presence of diverse constituents in a multicultural and pluralistic society.
Having alienated a number of crucial groups from its ranks, The Republican tent has shrunken dramatically over the last decade. With the changing demographics in the country, no viable politics can be about a dwindling, ageing white population, or an assortment of rabid

evangelicals, gay haters, and pro-life ideologues driven by blatant misogynistic tendencies. Neither can it be about pushing the poor and needy to the periphery while pandering to the rich. It will take some time for the Republican Party to change this image of itself, but it is within the realm of possibility to do so, if the right leaders emerge.

4. Prove that it is not the party of the rich or one beholden only to powerful, sectoral interests.

This will be a very difficult one to achieve as it has now become almost permanently entrenched in the minds of many Americans that the Republican Party caters only to the rich and does not care much about the needs of poor people. This has become more than a perception in the mind of the ordinary person; for many it is what the party has become. Without a seismic shift in the thinking of the party this image will only become further cemented in the minds of people thus alienating it from large blocks of voters who only want to be given a fair chance to make it up the social and economic ladder.

It will be very difficult for the party to overcome the perception that the Democrats have a greater love and concern for the poor than do Republicans. Republican criticism of programs directed to help the poor is part of an initiative to blunt this perception. But decades of Medicare, Medicaid, Social Security, and important safety net programs have carefully cemented in the minds of people that Democrats really do care more. This has made the constituency of the poor, voiceless and marginalized almost an unassailable citadel for Republicans. But this does not mean that they should not try to win friends and influence people in that constituency. Stupidly, however, Republicans seem resolutely content to let this image continue to define them. From the proposed Ryan Budget in the House, to the heartless gutting of important social safety net programs for the poor in states controlled by Republicans, the party is demonstrating a certain comfort level with a status quo that punishes people for falling on hard times. In the name of cost-saving, deficit reduction and tight budgetary constraints, they have eliminated programs for struggling Americans while hypocritically preserving and even adding to programs that benefit the rich and well connected. They often do this by stealth making sure that they do not reveal their true intentions when campaigning for office. They have demonstrated in no uncertain terms that they are detached from the day to day struggle of the ordinary American who they often treat with contempt. The party is no longer a compassionate party. One may justifiably criticize President George W. Bush for many things but he at least gave us compassionate conservatism and left an AIDS support legacy in Africa that is still commendable. What is the overarching philosophy that defines the party today? What are the leading spokespersons of the party offering to convince the American electorate that they stand for something other than a mindless obstruction of the governmental process?

Without an overarching philosophy of governance, many Americans have simply concluded that the federal government is rigged, that it has been taken over by special interest and lobby groups, that congressional representatives can be bought for a dime, and that there is no deep, philosophical moral basis that defines governance. This is true of both Democrats and Republicans. No single party has a monopoly on corruption or even stupidity which undermines good governance, but people are wont to blame the Republicans more for the corruption of government which they believe has become all too common in Washington.

5. End the hegemony of the Tea Party.

The Tea Party is largely a grassroots movement that came into existence in the summer of 2009 as a reaction against the Obama healthcare reform efforts. The nation was gripped by the ferocity of the reaction to the impending bill and with how quickly this ferocity caught on from one state to the next. At the beginning there was no discernible leadership of the movement, but there soon emerged leading spokespersons such as Congresswoman Michelle Bachmann and retired congressman Dick Armey who gave some legitimacy to it.

Any unbiased assessment of the Tea Party will admit that the movement represented a legitimate protest against a legislation about which a growing number of Americans had become uncomfortable. If one can set aside for a moment the movement's insultive caricature of the president, or the incendiary and at times intimidating rhetoric that characterized its genesis, there can be agreement for a certain degree of legitimacy for the movement. By the time of the 2010 mid-term elections, there were a number of Tea Party members who were ready to contest seats in the Congress and some state offices. It is an impressive fact of recent American political history how quickly the movement evolved into a credible political force having found favor with a large constituency of voters throughout the country. When the elections were held, a sizeable number were elected to Congress. This changed the political balance particularly in the House where the Republican Party won control and John Boehner replaced Nancy Pelosi as Speaker. However, the greatest consequence of this new won power was the seismic shift it caused in Republican politics.

Flushed with victory, the Tea Party representatives were seized with a mission which largely translated into whittling down the size of government, obstructing spending on the part of the federal government and resisting any notion of tax increases. In the latter they found a willing companion in Grover Norquist and his Americans for Tax Reform which had already placed most congressional Republicans under the tyranny of its tax orthodoxy. The tea partiers saw their victory as an endorsement of this platform. What caught a number of people by surprise was the almost fanatical commitment they brought to their mission. The first great test of this commitment was the debate on the nation's debt ceiling toward the end of 2011. It was soon realized that the Tea Party that arose out of the outrage against the pending Affordable Care Act in 2009 was not the Tea Party that came to Washington. They did not dilute their resentment for the legislation which they vowed to repeal, but their eyes were set on larger goals. They now had political power to achieve these objectives.

While not admitting it openly, it was clear that the more moderate Republicans (to the extent that any of these exist) were astounded at the ferocity with which these newcomers to the Congress sought to carry out their activities. They were clearly a force to be reckoned with as they had a sizeable group in the House that could tip the balance in any legislation going forward. Members of the old guard soon found themselves tripping over each other not sure whether they should endorse some of the more outrageous suggestions coming from the group or whether they should resist or criticize these platforms and reap the ire of deep-seated conservatives in the Republican base. There was no doubt that the Tea Party platform had great resonance with the base of the party. Most importantly, their views resonated with what many perceived as the need to restore the purity of conservative ideology which many believed had been severely eroded in the party.

Like Norquist and his pledge, Tea Party enthusiasts are fanatically committed to purist conservative ideology and see it as their mission to restore the altars that had been broken down over the years. They have pursued this mission with religious zeal to the extent that their beliefs have morphed into a rigid, doctrinaire philosophy that has become a matter of concern even for mainstream Republicans. President Obama is caricatured as the arch-enemy, or, in keeping with the religious analogy, the anti-Christ, of this purist, conservative thinking. His actions have to be resisted at all costs. Although there is not a strong glue of communication binding them together, the tea partiers have joined common cause with their Republican colleagues to make Mr. Obama a one-term President. Although they have not succeeded in their mission, they have not been averse to obstructing his legislative agenda and making it difficult for him to govern. Their scorched-earth obstruction of his policies is to ensure that he will not get anything done even if the country is hurt in the process. It is not that they oppose on the basis of well thought out positions based on the well-established traditional principles and philosophy of compromise, but that leading lights in the party are committed to make him fail as a matter of policy.

It was damnable to hear a Republican leader in the most deliberative body in the world, The US Senate, declare for the world to hear that the number one priority of his party would be to ensure that the president did not get another term. This followed upon the fulminations coming from the High Priest of Obama vitriol, Rush Limbaugh, extolling similar sentiments. This crass political declaration by Mr. McConnell was unworthy of him as a leader in the senate, but detrimental to a party which did not oppose this view. In keeping with its self-imposed mandate to hurt the president politically, the party has become further radicalized along rigid ideological lines and this pretty much accounts for the gridlock in the Congress today.

In their mission to obstruct, Tea Party members have demonstrated a zealotry that has not been seen in the Congress for a long time. The specific intention of the Tea Party caucus that was formed under Congresswoman Bachmann's leadership ensured that the agenda to oppose the president at all costs, with whatever venom available, was pursued. Not only must the "socialist" president be stopped, but any bill with which they did not find favor must be resisted even if it came from their own Republican colleagues. This has led to unacknowledged tension between the young radicals and the older, traditional wing of the party. This tension boiled over recently when the respected Republican veteran, John McCain, had to upbraid the obstreperous newcomer from Texas, Ted Cruz. Recent posturing on the part of some Republicans in the senate, especially with regard to comprehensive immigration reform, indicate a certain impatience on the part of Senate Republicans to get back to how government can function on behalf of the people. These Republicans have seen the modus operandi of the Tea Party, and while they have not distanced themselves fully from its platform, many of the more moderate members who have not aligned themselves fully with Tea Party posturing, recognize that they are fast becoming a party of obsolescence.

This was brought into sharp relief by the latest round of government shutdown and debt ceiling debacle which stunned many people in the country and the international community. Senators like John McCain and Lindsey Graham have enough experience and political common-sense to know that the party will lose significant traction if they do not arrest the rot represented by the extreme posturing of a Ted Cruz, Mike Lee or Marco Rubio. This is why McCain has stepped up his criticisms especially of Cruz and Lee, and why, in finding common cause with Democrats, seems to be deliberately sidelining the more rabid positions of Tea Party mavens.

This is at it should be if the Republican Party is to become again a credible force in American politics. The political extremism represented by the Tea Party should worry reform minded Republicans and those who still believe in the spirit of compromise as an essential ingredient of good governance. It should also concern those who want to see a vibrant, democratic process in our politics and who recognize the importance of the Republican brand to that process. The extremism we have seen of late can only serve to further alienate the Republican Party from the mainstream of American politics.

John Boehner and the 113th Congress

Admittedly, Tea Party obduracy is particularly worse in the House than in the Senate. There the party has taken petulance to a new level to the extent that it has become an essential hallmark, an important governing principle, of how the party conducts the people's business. The Speaker, John Boehner, seems out of his depth as to how to deal with them. A reasonable man who no doubt wants the best for the country, he has allowed himself to become captive to the wishes of the Tea Party. In the face of their dangerous posturing that could affect the health of the country, he has proved himself impotent to stand up and lead against their more outrageous demands. The latest outrage was his capitulation to this radical group which resulted in the shutdown of the government and the near default of the country on its debt obligations. Mr. Boehner himself admitted that shutting down the government in an attempt to defund the Affordable Care Act was not a winnable strategy, yet he failed dismally to act forcefully in enforcing discipline on this unruly bunch when the situation demanded it. Neither has he been able to forge compromise as he would have done before the Tea Party came to Congress. Presently, he seems to have resigned himself to the political fatalism that he cannot do much, while blaming the president and members of the Democratic Party for not getting bills passed. Those that have been passed have been done on a largely partisan basis which Mr. Boehner and his fellow Republicans know would not reach the President's desk. Instead of seeking bipartisan consensus, bills have been pushed through the House that will hurt vulnerable populations, lower environmental standards, and limit the chances for those seeking jobs. No time has been spent seriously discussing jobs or the country's crumbling infrastructure. Yet, the country is bracing for the gladiatorial battle that will ensue when the decision to

> *When he genuflected to the Tea Party, Mr. Boehner proved himself to be a weak leader and a man unworthy of the office he holds.*

continue funding the government and raise its borrowing limits has to be fully engaged in the future.

The truth is that with regard to the 113th Congress, the Speaker has presided over the most lackluster House in recent memory. He has wasted precious legislative hours trying to repeal the landmark healthcare legislation which has received the imprimatur of the Supreme Court and is now the settled law of the land. Mr. Boehner has allowed himself to be bamboozled by the Tea Party to oppose the legislation even though he has admitted that it is settled law and ought to be respected as such. When he genuflected to the Tea Party, Mr. Boehner proved himself to be a weak leader and a man unworthy of the office he holds. His recent attempts at cosmetic opposition to Tea Party groups have not changed this opinion in any significant way. His pandering to Tea Party radicalism and his reluctant acquiescence to their demands, are to a large extent responsible for the poor rating that the American people continue to give Congress and especially the House under his leadership.

The Republican Party will continue to atrophy and wither on the vines as long as it allows the Tea Party as a parasitic hybrid to continue sucking the life blood from it. As the battle for the soul of the party intensifies, the adults in the party must assume greater responsibility in rescuing it from the quarrelsome and cantankerous party that it has fast become; a party that listens more to its own voice and which, as a result, fails to hear the voice of the people. The 2014 mid-term elections will be a litmus test of where the people really are with Tea Party posturing. There is every indication that people are growing increasingly impatient with their shenanigans as more and more they are being seen as spurs on the heels of the nation's progress.

6. End the Norquist Tax Orthodoxy

Having been whipped by the expiration of the Bush tax cuts in January 2013, it is amazing that Grover Norquist, the purveyor of the notorious tax pledge, continues to exercise influence over an overwhelming majority of Republicans in Congress and state houses. It is true that his influence has diminished, but the fact that so many are still signatories to his tax pledge clearly indicates how readily members of the party are prepared to bend their minds to the tyranny of an idea. The pledge may very well go the way of the dinosaurs, but Norquist is a shrewd operator and it would be a mistake to underestimate the exaggerated influence he has over the party and his ability to weave radical ideology into legislative policy. To survive, one can expect him to strengthen the alliance between his organization and Tea Party radicals as symbiotically they seek to turn the party into an ultra right entity. The intention will be to have a presidential candidate from this group for the 2016 elections.

Norquist's pledge was introduced during the Reagan Administration to protect the low marginal tax rates of the Reagan Tax Reform Act of 1986. The Americans for Tax Reform functioned as a watchdog for these reforms, but over the years its method of enforcing compliance through the tax pledge has grown very rigid. Some would argue that it has become a monolithic organization whose rigid adherence to the doctrine of "no new taxes" has led many to discount whatever noble intentions it may have possessed at the time of its founding.

Since the pledge was introduced, Norquist has had remarkable success in getting elected leaders, largely Republicans, to sign up. So important has the pledge become that by the time of the G. W Bush Administration it was taken as a matter of fact that it was political suicide not to sign it and having signed not to live up to its rigid contours. It may be granted that many who have signed it believe in the philosophy that it is not good for the economy to raise taxes on people; that the best approach is to cut spending instead of raising taxes on job creators. Some may even believe that signing the pledge is what Republicans did; that it was a basic covenant that one made with the people as a Republican candidate for office; that it is un-Republican not to sign it. These may be noble intentions consistent with what may be defined as conservative values, but many will not admit that the most prominent reason that they sign is fear that Norquist can organize primary challenges against any person who does not sign, or having signed, reneges on it. This fear has been like the sword of Damocles over the heads of Republican politicians.

In the past, Norquist has been very adept in carrying out this threat. Careers of lawmakers have been cut short by Norquist's organization coming against them in primaries. Perhaps the most poignant example in the 2012 elections was the defeat of Richard Lugar, the long serving, affable and competent senator from Indiana. When George H.W. Bush ran in 1988 he had signed the pledge and had committed to not raising taxes in that now famous or infamous "read my lips" declaration. When he came to office he immediately raised the top tax rate to 31 percent and added surtaxes to jets, luxury sedans and yachts. In other words, he soaked the rich. He had seen the importance of restraining the soaring federal deficit. As it turned out, his actions in this regard were correct. It is not farfetched to suggest that his decision helped to spur the recovery of the economy which had begun when Clinton took office in 1992. Bush lost the election for lack of robust support from his base because he was seen to have gone back on the pledge. This strengthened Norquist's hand and concretized in the minds of Republican politicians that once the pledge is signed it should not be broken under any condition or circumstance.

But since the November 2012 elections cracks have appeared in Norquist's well crafted designs on the Republican Party. An increasing number of those who signed have distanced themselves from the pledge, some disavowing it altogether. Of note are Senators Lindsey Graham, Saxby Chambliss and Bob Corker including Peter King from the House. A mass stampede has not yet occurred, but it is becoming clear that a growing number of legislators are realizing that an obligatory commitment to a tax orthodoxy is not necessarily a good thing for the country. In any event, the election results vindicated the Democratic Party in its insistence that taxes must be raised on the rich two percent of the population. This was accomplished with the expiration of the Bush tax cuts in January 2013. This should have been the key that unlocked the handcuff that Norquist and his organization had placed around the wrists of the pledge signers. How many will be bold enough to walk away into freedom is anyone's guess.

The ending of the Bush tax cuts may have been the greatest blow to the survival of the Americans for Tax Reform. It may very well have signaled the beginning of the end of Norquist's influence in Washington. But no one should write him off. As a survivor he has a remarkable ability to adapt to any changing environment. He will evolve into something new. Expect him to strengthen his relationship with the Tea Party as they team up to suck the lifeblood out of a dying, fractious Republican Party. One suspects that he is working feverishly behind the scenes to deepen and strengthen this alliance. If one's suspicions are correct then one can expect a hardening of the already rigid positions being taken by the Tea Party in their battle with more moderate elements in the Republican camp. What is clear is that the rigid commitment to no tax increases will continue for this has become an important conduit for the rich and powerful to maintain influence over tax policy. But at some point the moderates in the party will have to make a distinction between their commitment to a pledge or their fear of Tea Party obduracy and their commitment to their Oath of Office which requires them to serve and protect the best interests of the people of the United States.

Norquist and his supporters will of course argue that there is no discrepancy between their commitment to their Oath and not raising taxes; that both merely complement each other. But we have seen over time that those who sign the pledge are more ardent in their support of it than they are of clear demands to do something good for the country. The existential threat of being driven from office overrides their moral commitment to their Oath to the American people. The important thing to note here is the ultimate travesty that their duty under the Constitution is trumped by their fealty to special interest groups. It is failure to appreciate this distinction which could lead the Republican Party to do great harm to the country as happened in the downgrade of our sovereign debt. To the extent that the pledge is seen to be more sacrosanct than their duties and responsibilities as elected officials under the Constitution, the actions of those who sign the pledge may at best be considered injurious to the public good and at worse treasonous.

The first duty of elected officials is to protect and preserve the Constitution and then to demonstrate the kind of leadership that puts the interest of the people at the very center of their concern. Those who deliberately fail to carry out their duties under the Constitution out of fear of being driven out of office are cowards and do not deserve to hold elected office. And this applies to both sides of the political spectrum. By putting personal ambition above service to country they prove themselves to be traitors to the country's democratic way of life.

Norquist and others like him are able to enjoy the influence they do in Washington because politicians who purport to have their constituents' interests at heart have abdicated their responsibilities in order to retain power. Norquist and his rich backers fit neatly into this psychology of power and actually revel in the prestige and perhaps wealth that it brings them. Never in recent times have the rich had it so good and never in the past decade has Norquist and his organization enjoyed such power and influence in Washington. When asked by a largely slobbering press about the power he has, Norquist is fond of telling his fawning hosts that he has no power; that it belongs to the people who the lawmakers will have to contend with if they dare to go against the pledge. In trying to be self-deprecatory, Norquist reveals a man intoxicated with power and elated at the thought that so many men and women in the halls of power could be under his thrall. He only has to say the word "primary" and those with "impure thoughts" who would dare to question his pledge fall back in line. They may not know the level of contempt he has for them. It may be contempt not unlike that which Jack Abramoff, a man who also enjoyed pervasive influence in the halls of Congress before his demise, held out for congressional lawmakers whom he bribed or otherwise influenced to do his bidding.

There has been a tendency on the part of Norquist's detractors to demonize him or to even envy him for the prestige he enjoys. His organization has been called "a nefarious" organization. Even David Stockman who served as President Reagan's budget director, once described him as a "fiscal policy terrorist." [8] Uncomplimentary descriptions of him have come from the social progressive movement and from the left of center of the political spectrum. But none of this has dissuaded Norquist from his mission which he pursues with fanatical zeal. He is the quintessential gadfly who is not dissuaded by criticisms. If anything, criticisms have only emboldened and kept him in the spotlight. As long as he is able to sustain the attention of the press the longer he will remain in the public consciousness as a lonely crusader against governmental tax tyranny. So while they pillory him and give him a hard time his critics do not realize that they may be doing him a favor by contributing to his longevity.

While Norquist may be blamed for his tax rigidity, his tyrannical grip on the Republican Party is a blame that belongs solely to those members. He would never be able to exercise the influence he has without the willing complicity of those members who have outsourced their loyalty and perhaps their brains to him. Although he uses it as a fig leaf behind which he hides his true intentions, Norquist is right that lawmakers are accountable to their constituents. It is the voter and not Norquist who has the real power. He may run a primary challenge against a candidate or spend millions to get a candidate elected as was done in the last presidential elections, but he has no more power than the lonely voter who stands in that voting booth and makes his mark for democracy. And the American voter has a greater sense of fairness than one would allow. Most know when they are being jerked around. If a reasonable argument can be advanced why there should be a tax increase he or she can be persuaded of this as the polls have shown repeatedly. It therefore befuddles the mind that Republican candidates fail to grasp this even at a time when the polls before and after the last elections showed that over 60 percent of the people are for tax increases on the wealthiest segment of the population.

Caught between the extremes of Norquist's tax zealotry on the one hand and the Tea Party's fiscal obduracy on the other, the Republican Party is between the proverbial rock and a hard place. The options it faces may be just iced teas and frozen cakes. There is no great prospect that the party will break out of this mould anytime soon. If anything, recent posturing would suggest a tendency for greater ideological rigidity within the party. This can only worsen as the dash towards the next presidential primaries begins. It is becoming clearer by the day that the people want an end to the incivility that has characterized the nation's politics over the past five years. They want an end to the rigid commitment to political dogma which feeds this incivility.

If the Republican Party wants to be taken seriously as a credible force in the American political consciousness, part of its rebranding must be the repudiation of this doctrinaire approach to politics. A large part of this will be determined by how successful it will be in expunging the Tea Party from its system, and how demonstrable will be the Tea Party's ability to cling to or even alter the DNA of its host. The party must reposition itself to become a credible part of the dialogue for change or allow itself to become more calloused and irrelevant to this conversation. To be a relevant part of the conversation and thus being relevant to the future of American politics, there are two important imperatives that the party will need to embrace. These will be addressed in the next two chapters.

··

Notes on Chapter One

1. Chris Wallace *Fox News Sunday*, May 26, 2013

2. Governor Bobby Jindal, *GOP Needs Action, Not Navel-gazing*, June 18, 2013.

3. Interview on *The Ed Show*, MSNBC, October 27, 2012.

4. Interview on *Andrea Mitchell Reports*, MSNBC, October 4, 2012.

5. *Fox News Live* news program aired on November 5, 2012.

6. Address to the 2012 Democratic National Convention held in Charlotte, North Carolina, September 4-6, 2012.

7. William Kristol, *Weekly Standard,* December 17, 2012.

8. Lloyd Grove: *The Dark Lord of the Debt Mess*, **The Dailybeast.com**, August 9 2011.

CHAPTER TWO

THE IMMIGRATION IMPERATIVE

*Send us your huddled masses, yearning to be free-***Emma Lazarus**

<<<<<<>>>>>

A nyone who has had even a brief acquaintance with the immigration crisis in America will concede that this is one of the most pressing issues that the country has to contend with at this time. The issue has forced itself upon the national agenda in a way that few issues have. In any prominent national polling, immigration repeatedly appears among the top three problems that Americans are concerned about. It was a hotly debated topic in the just ended presidential election and no doubt figured prominently in the defeat of Mitt Romney, the Republican contender. Again, the Republican Party found itself on the wrong side of this issue.

The last big attempt at immigration reform in 2006 ended in disarray. President Bush meant well in getting comprehensive immigration reform but his efforts were neutralized even by members of his own party who considered the measures too radical and far reaching. On both sides of the political fence immigration has become a significant part of a political chess game that is being played in Washington. This is tragic for the issue is impatient of resolution and Americans are becoming increasingly restless at the recalcitrance they see and the seeming impotence of their representatives to deal creatively with the problem.

There are a number of truisms about immigration that can be noted at the outset. A powerful one is that since immigration began in earnest in the 1800's, America has benefitted tremendously from the talent, genius and expertise of those who have left distant lands to come to its shores. People came because America provided a route to prosperity which was a distant dream in the countries from which they migrated. They had one interest which superseded all others: to make a better life for themselves and their families. America held out great hope for them, the hope that they could eke out a living in a land of freedom and opportunity. They believed that if they worked hard and were disciplined enough they could make it. For many around the world this dream is still alive.

Once immigrants arrived in America they knew instinctively that they had landed in a land of opportunity. They only needed government to create an environment in which they could thrive, an environment of fairness, of justice where people played by the same rules and where there were no impediments in the path of individual progress. They only wanted to realize their God-given potentials and to release the power for greatness that many knew they possessed. Many have realized their potentials and many more will continue to do so.

If there is anything to define America as an exceptional nation it is simply its ability to absorb people from every culture in the world. People are not lining up to go to other nations as they do to come to America. They are not risking life and property to get to other nations as they do to reach America. There has to be something exceptional going on in America that pulls them. This important reality is often lost in the often acrimonious debate on immigration. Absent is a sense of history of how America became an immigrant nation; that the first Europeans who came were seeking a land of freedom in which they could practice their religion without fear. They were driven by the principle that the power of self-determination was best realized in a context of human freedom, not under the capricious will of a monarchical system or dictator. In fashioning their manifest destiny, they were not prepared to yield any ground to those who might have wished to frustrate their inherent right to self-determination. It is this principle of self-determination, buttressed by the inherent right to be free, that later became the bedrock principle on which the Constitution was founded.

No one better understood the pulse of America as an immigrant nation than Abraham Lincoln. In trying to define who the immigrant is today, it is useful to refer to a speech that he gave on July 10, 1858. At the time that Lincoln gave the speech the nation was only thirty years old with just about thirty million people. Today the population is over ten times greater but even then immigration was a vexing issue. If the challenge was great then, consider where the country is today.

Lincoln began by acknowledging that America is a mighty nation. He paid homage to the Founding Fathers whom he referred to as the "iron men." He acknowledged his generation's gratitude to them for their sacrifice and foresight and sought to connect the new immigrants from Europe with the Founding Fathers. The passage of time and the birth of new generations might have thinned the blood line, but the connection, he conceded, cannot be made through genetics; but through the Declaration of Independence, an overarching moral principle that linked the hearts of liberty loving people everywhere. He said:

> But when they look through that old Declaration of Independence they find that those old men say that 'We hold these truths to be self-evident, that all men are created equal,' and then they feel that that moral sentiment taught in that day evidences their relation to these men, that it is the father of all moral principle in them, and that they have a right to claim it as though they were blood of the blood, and flesh of the men who wrote that Declaration, (loud and long applause) and so they are. That is the electric cord in that declaration that links the hearts of patriotic and liberty-loving men together that will link those patriotic hearts as long as the love of freedom exists.in the minds of men throughout the world[1] (applause).

While the love of freedom had universal appeal, America's desire to absorb those who wanted to be free gave it a special standing among the nations of the world. Lincoln was clear that the overriding principle that knit the immigrant with the American native was the equality of men and their desire to be free. There was no equivocation where this was concerned. For him it was more than a philosophical statement. It was a pragmatic one founded on the basic love for freedom and all that it entailed. Thus, he could insist that those born in America had no more sacred claim on the desire to be free than those who chose to come here. What drew the long and sustained applause was the audience's concurrence with Lincoln that the same patriotic loyalties that inflamed the Founding Fathers was no less the flame that burns in the hearts of those who risk all to come to these blessed shores. They must be afforded the same generosity when they arrive as were afforded these "iron men" and their descendants. Lincoln's appeal for a generous regard for the immigrant was deeply rooted in the moral sentiments contained in the founding documents which embraced freedom. It was not freedom as an abstract statement but that which related to the existential struggle of people everywhere for self-determination and personal progress.

It is still this general sentiment that ought to define America's approach to the immigration problem today. It is heartening that despite the vitriol that often accompanies the immigration debate, it is fair to say that most Americans are open to the idea of immigration and would agree with Lincoln's sentiments regarding the matter. It has now become palpably clear that most Americans want to have the problem fixed in a just and comprehensive manner. They do not want unfettered immigration where great swathes of people can live in the country without documentation. But they do not want an approach that merely tinkers with the problem and which does not address it wholesomely. They know almost instinctively that if the problem is not fixed the country's security over the long term will be jeopardized. The humbug is whether there is the political will and leadership that can command the moral fortitude to do the right and decent thing in enacting appropriate legislation that is fair and just and which can correct the problem well into the foreseeable future.

A Brief Review of Presidential Approaches to the Immigration Problem

President Reagan

In 1986 President Reagan signed the *Immigration Reform and Control Act* which legalized close to 3 million undocumented persons. Greater border enforcement was emphasized along with sanctions against those who knowingly employed illegal workers. The legalization of undocumented persons was considered an amnesty program by those who opposed the measure. The belief at the time was that the Act would open the floodgates to other undocumented persons to pour into the country through the porous southern border.

In his farewell address to the nation on January 11, 1989, immigration was on the President's mind as he described America as the shining city on a hill. He said:

> *In my mind it was a tall, proud city built on rocks stronger than oceans, windswept, God-blessed and teeming with people of all kinds living in harmony and peace; a city with free ports that hummed with commerce and creativity. And if there had to be city walls, the walls had doors and the doors were open to anyone with the will and heart to get here.*[2]

Reagan's genius resided in his ability to let the nation feel good about itself and he did not disappoint in this speech. It was expansive as it was inclusive and came close to what Lincoln would have endorsed. Since the Reagan initiative successive administrations have sought to address the problem with varying degrees of success. It is a shame that since that time there has been no comprehensive reform of immigration.

President Clinton

The Clinton administration was at best lethargic in addressing what had fast become a difficult problem to solve. Clinton believed in a policy that was open and non-dogmatic. But his efforts at reform were dogged by a combative Republican Party that had gained control of the Congress in the 1994 mid-term elections. They charged that immigration was being used as a political tool to bolster the president's chances at the polls. The charge was not farfetched as the president won re-election in 1996 when many undocumented persons who had become citizens under his watch were able to vote for the first time. In 1996 he signed the *Illegal Immigration Reform and Immigrant Responsibility Act.* Under this initiative more border patrol agents were deployed to the southern border and sanctions were strengthened against employers who hired undocumented persons.

Clinton's efforts were hardly an improvement on Reagan's. Undocumented persons continued to swarm across the southern border. The promise to secure the border has been tepid and southern states with borders with Mexico have been overburdened by waves of undocumented persons in their cities.

President George W. Bush

By the time President George W Bush came to office, the problem had reached crisis proportions with the violence from the drug trade threatening to undermine civil society in towns and cities bordering Mexico. Despite his party's control of the White House and Congress until 2006, the Bush administration failed to carry out any meaningful reform of immigration. It was not that Bush did not have a broad set of ideas that lent plausibility and credibility to improving the situation, but he failed to get the support of quite a number of Republicans in the Congress. In an address to the nation on May 15, 2006, Bush spelt out his views on immigration reform. He believed that the country must first secure its borders but must remain open to trade and legal immigration while at the same time shutting out illegal immigrants, terrorists and criminals. He further believed that there should be a temporary worker program which would allow foreign workers to enter the country for a limited time to work. This program would match willing foreign workers with willing American employers for jobs Americans were not doing or did not seem willing to do. Employers would be held accountable for people they employed under an electronic verification process.

Recognizing that millions of undocumented persons were already in the country, Bush's policy would seek to have them documented though not providing them with an automatic path to citizenship. He recognized that it was untenable to round up millions of people and deport them. He stressed that this would not be an Amnesty program as was the charge against Reagan's policy. Those who would wish to be documented would pay a meaningful penalty, pay taxes, learn English and work in a job for a number of years. Those who met these requirements would be able to apply for citizenship but they would have to wait in line behind those who have played by the rules and obeyed the law. They would have paid their debt to society and demonstrated the character of good citizenship. In time they would be assimilated into the society and realize their dreams thus renewing the American spirit and contributing to the country's progress.

Bush's hope for a sensible approach to an intractable problem was dashed to pieces by a senate controlled by Democrats. The bill was killed along party lines. There was even lack of support from Republicans in both Houses who viewed the bill as providing another amnesty program which they strenuously resented. They were not prepared to reward illegal immigrants as Reagan was seen to have done. In the end, Bush was forced to give only token help to border security by signing the *Border Security Act* in October 2006. The main provision of this bill was the building of a 700 mile fence on the southern border with Mexico. He sent 6000 National Guard personnel to the area to assist the Border Patrol with surveillance technology and enhanced intelligence gathering capabilities. Comprehensive immigration reform would have represented Bush's signature achievement but he was denied the opportunity to realize it. With the disaster and chaos of his war in Iraq, culminating in the great recession towards the end of his tenure in 2008, passing the immigration bill would have been a moment of redemption for him. One can imagine his sadness at this not being done. He was clearly on the right side of the immigration debate but fate seemed to have robbed him of his significant moment in history.

President Obama

I have given some detail to the Bush policy not because it failed but because I believe it was a rational attempt to deal with an existential problem that had become even more impatient of resolution. Also, a careful look at the proposals of Bush and Obama will indicate that there is congruence in the positions they advocate on the immigration issue. For his first term, President Obama campaigned on a platform that promised comprehensive immigration reform. The exigencies of the recession and his perceived need to reform healthcare largely pushed the immigration issue to the back burner. This was a disappointment for the Hispanic community that had voted overwhelmingly for him in the 2008 elections. Having won the second term, again with tremendous help from the Hispanic community which gave him 73 percent of that community's vote, there are high expectations that he will deliver on his promise this time around. He is still hobbled by a weak economy, but the Hispanic and other communities will not be in a forgiving mood if a bill is not signed for comprehensive immigration reform by 2014.

The broad outline of the President's policy incorporates elements of what comprehensive immigration reform ought to embrace. What are these basic elements?

Border Security

In a number of speeches the President has been quite clear that strengthening security on America's borders has to be an integral part of any policy to reform immigration. It is important that this be so for immigration today represents a graver security matter than it ever did prior to the terrorist attack on America. Sometimes the conversation about border security largely revolves around what is happening on the country's southern border, but it is a matter that affects every point of entry into the country. The Department of Homeland Security has given unprecedented resources to border security.

Undocumented Workers.
The president believes that businesses should be held responsible for breaking the law and for exploiting undocumented workers they employ by paying them low, degrading wages. This behavior is not only inhumane but undermines the compensation of legitimate American workers. The lack of enforcement of this aspect of the immigration laws has been a large contributor to the defective immigration system that currently operates in the country. At the center of this deficiency are large swathes of undocumented persons who come across the border seeking employment often at the urging of those who currently operate illegally in the system. Some who come on temporary visitor and student visas simply disappear at the end of their stay or study.

The president has been very adamant that businesses must bear the core of the responsibility to verify that people in their employ are in the country legitimately. The Electronic Employment Verification Program, or E-verify for short, was introduced by the Bush Administration to enable employers to easily and quickly verify the work authorization of workers. Bush's Executive Order which enabled this specified that this should apply to all workers, but the Obama administration has scaled this back to include only new employees. This has led to the charge that the administration has not been robust in dealing with illegal employees at the workplace.

Notwithstanding this criticism, the Obama administration has been resolute in rounding up and deporting undocumented persons through US Immigration and Customs Enforcement (ICE). According to the Department of Homeland Security, as of July 2012, the Obama administration has deported 1.4 million illegal immigrants. Priority is given to the deportation of criminal immigrants. There seems to be reluctance on the part of the administration to deport undocumented workers though some have been caught up in "quiet" raids on workplaces. The administration appears less strident in prosecuting employers of undocumented workers.

Pathway to Citizenship

Recognizing that the system is broken and needs to be fixed, there is a raging debate about what is to be done with the almost 12 million undocumented persons who are already living in the United States. This is not an easy problem to solve and the federal government has to admit its own culpability in the situation being as it is. The truth is that immigration laws have not been robustly enforced. Notwithstanding this there is growing acknowledgment that it is of no practical value for the government to set out on a mission to round up and deport the millions of undocumented persons who are in the country. Not only would this be expensive, but it could involve employing tactics that are frankly un-American such as breaking up families and uprooting many who have already assimilated into the country and who are making worthwhile contributions to society. It is not just a moral problem that the country faces in the breakup of families and its attendant problems, but an economic one. Mass deportation would be very costly, not only in the capital expended in carrying out the deportation, but in the cost to the economy in the dislocation of these persons from the important economic functions they presently perform to their families and the wider society.

In addressing this problem the Obama administration is open to holding those living in the country illegally responsible for their actions. This would mean, among other things, requiring undocumented persons to register and undergo national security and criminal background checks, paying a penalty and taxes and learning English. They would also have to wait in line behind those who have already applied for citizenship. In creating this pathway there need not be any contradiction between enforcing the laws of the country and giving legal immigration status to those who seek it. It should not be an open-ended process but one defined by carefully worked out practical timelines. The process must be open and fair and justly reflect the values of a welcoming society.

It is in the context of America as a welcoming society that the Development, Relief and Education of Alien Minors Act, better known as the DREAM Act, was introduced. The legislation was intended to help young people who were brought to the United States by undocumented parents as children and who were now graduating from high school, to become legal residents and finally citizens. This would allow them to continue living in America and continue with their education in college and beyond. There were strict guidelines to adhere to but at least a door was opened which was not there before. Different versions of the Act have been discussed since 2001 when it was first introduced to the House by Representative Luis Gutierrez from California. From that time until 2011 it has undergone various modifications and finally suffered filibuster fatigue in the Senate.

On June 15, 2012 President Obama, by executive authority, instructed the Department of Homeland Security to no longer deport young undocumented immigrants who met certain criteria previously mentioned in the DREAM Act. This was the most important immigration initiative by the administration to date and was part response to the growing disenchantment of the Latino community after he failed to pass immigration reform as promised in the 2008 campaign. The program will last for two years at a time and will have to be ratified or incorporated as part of a larger comprehensive reform thrust.

Strengthening Economic Competitiveness

There is an emerging consensus that it makes no practical sense to train bright minds in our universities in the skills required by 21st century economic competitiveness and then at the end of the training period declare those people unwelcomed in the society. Not only is this a foolhardy, but it robs the country of the minds and talents that are necessary to build America into the highly innovative and technologically sound society that it ought to be. Part of the president's plan is to find a way to absorb this talented pool of young people that are needed for present and new industries. An innovative immigration policy should provide an opening for people to be allowed to work temporarily in the country at jobs for which US workers are not available.

Moving Forward

There are important points to be made on either side of the political debate on immigration. The subject did not figure prominently in the recently concluded presidential campaign. It was clear where the president stood since he had to address it at various stages in his first term. His incursion into the DREAM Act proposals is a case in point. It is not clear where the Republicans stand on the issue for apart from a hodge-podge of views there is not a coherent policy to have come from that party since the Bush attempt at a comprehensive legislation in 2007. The few times he was forced to address the issue, candidate Mitt Romney was very incoherent and gave the impression that it was a subject he would rather not address. In his rambling comments on immigration it became quite clear that it was a subject he was not comfortable talking about. This might have explained his infamous comment on self-deportation which itself was not clearly defined or articulated. The question could be raised as to whether Romney himself understood the full import of what he advocated. Throughout his long campaign to win the White House, there was no substance given to what he believed a decent immigration policy should entail.

In addition to not having a coherent policy, spotty remarks by the Republican presidential candidate infuriated minority groups and alienated the important Latino voting bloc. The party was not seen to be friendly to immigrants and Mr. Romney's "47 percent" remarks did not endear him to many in the Asian and Hispanic communities. By their caustic rhetoric, Republican spokespersons left no doubt in the minds of many that these groups were not welcomed. Members of these groups felt that the Republicans could not be trusted to represent their best interests. Latinos especially resented the use of the term "illegal aliens", yet the party demonstrated no sensitivity to this fact. So insensitive were they that candidate Romney repeated the term at the important Latino forum put on by *Telemundo* television which gave him the opportunity to speak directly to the Hispanic community.

It should have been no surprise that President Obama received 73 percent of the Latino vote and Mr. Romney 21 percent. Republican candidates gave the impression that undocumented workers were an invading horde of welfare seekers who would become a drag on the country's resources. In the present debate on immigration there are some in the party and in influential conservative circles, like the Heritage Foundation, who have not moved far beyond this thinking.

While Republican senators such as Marco Rubio are prepared to make grudging concessions that can make a comprehensive reform bill possible, there are still those who demean immigrants as if they are of an "inferior specie" which will suck the life blood out of the nation. There is no integrity on their part to admit that large segments of this "inferior" demographic are making a worthwhile contribution to the society that they would gladly become citizens of. By their hard work they have earned consideration for benefits. What stands between them working and receiving benefits is their undocumented status. This is a situation that any well-thinking and just society would want to remedy.

By resurrecting the 47 percent myth, Republican politicians and their sympathizers in the conservative right, continue to hurt their cause by laboring under the illusion that minority communities are only interested in getting "stuff" and that they gravitate to the Democratic Party precisely for this reason. This is an insulting charge and one based upon falsehoods. An equally egregious analysis emerged from a Heritage Foundation supported study that the IQ of immigrants is inferior to that of their Caucasian counterparts. To the organization's credit it later dissociated itself from the study, but this was late in dissuading people of the view that such study is part of the diet of conservative ideology.

The study only served to strengthen the belief that the Republican Party is contemptuous of immigrants. Many see this as an essential characteristic of dysfunctional Republican politics. The party does not understand how resentful immigrants are of the charge that they come to America to be a burden to the state as welfare recipients. The truth is that immigrants are among the most hardworking people in America. A Pew Research Center study on Asian-American work attitudes reveals that this group has a healthy work ethic.[3] This is also true of many in other immigrant groups. Like any other group, there are some who fall through the cracks and have to be given governmental assistance. But they do not seek assistance as a matter of choice, but only when necessity is forced upon them and, even then, reluctantly.

Contrary to popular conservative thinking which also populates conservative media, they do not believe that they are entitled or that the government owes them anything. Entitlement is a code word for minority dependence that is thrown around by members of the Republican Party and the conservative press as if to suggest that it is only that population that craves government assistance. But the facts bear out that white poor people also share in these entitlement programs even more than do blacks or Hispanics. When the conservative media pontificate about entitlement programs or people's dependence upon government for "stuff", as Bill O'Reilly of *Fox News* likes to call it, one never gets the impression that they mean white people, but members of minority groups, especially the black community. But there are irrefutable statistics which indicate that there are more white people on food stamps than there are blacks; Hispanics are even less.

Asian and Latino American immigrants do not believe, as President Reagan did, that government is the problem. They see a role for government in the regulation of the economy, in security and in providing the environment in which people can thrive productively without hindrance. They also see a role for government in assistance being available to those who fall on hard times as happens in an economic crisis. For them this is not Western style socialism but what decent governments do. They do not believe that government should be intrusive in the lives of people, but they know that government has to be there to do what only governments can do. For them there is no concept of a Big Government or Small Government and certainly there is no government by "trickle down." Immigrants know instinctively that this is poppycock.

From Republican rhetoric you would think that government is irrelevant and ought to be relegated to the sidelines when it comes to the concerns of the poor and distressed minority groups. But it is okay when its resources can be stripped and doled out to the rich in tax cuts or subsidies to large oil companies that do not really need them. By their sour attitude to immigrants, Republicans push more immigrants into the arms of the Democrats than would otherwise be the case. And this is ironic, and at the same time sad, for the truth is that immigrant communities support a lot of the values of mainstream Republican politics such as non-intrusive government, strong families, patriotism, and hard work, to name a few. But they believe that the Democrats are more trustworthy when it comes to fairness and social justice. And social justice is not to be equated with entitlement or social progressivism as conservative ideology would suggest.

There is a great deal of work that Republicans have to do to get on the right side of the immigration debate. President G. W. Bush after Reagan was the last Republican president to set an appropriate tone of conviviality concerning immigration. This is why he won over 40 percent of the Hispanic vote in his re-election. He at least had a philosophy that governed his approach to the problem -compassionate conservatism. Never mind that this did not work for the Iraqis and the horrendous loss of American life and treasure. But the present approach of the Republicans to immigration is neither compassionate nor conservative in the traditional sense of the term. At least, many in the immigrant community do not sense that this is so. What they see is a party boiling in vitriol against those who would want to come here; a party that would build fences instead of bridges of friendship; and a party that does not resonate with their existential realities and which seems more than willing to deny them a seat at the table of brotherhood.

There is evidence that a wind of change has begun to blow in the party. More well-thinking Republicans led by Senator Marco Rubio, himself a son of immigrant parents and who grew up in a largely Hispanic immigrant community, are beginning to realize that they have to drastically change the narrative on immigration. The present narrative is too hostile to the central place of immigration in the building of an exceptional America. Instead, this narrative is inimical to people seeing America as an exceptional nation to which they can come with their families, work hard, become citizens and build out their part of the American dream. There can be no part of this narrative which supports the myopic and xenophobic rhetoric of those who would want to preserve a dying order and who indulge in rhetoric about balkanization.

The hope is not whether comprehensive immigration reform will happen, but how soon and what might be the content of the reform. Those in the Republican Party who are wise enough to understand the ramifications of these changes must begin the dialogue which can move that party to a better place. Wisdom would dictate that these changes be embraced but managed in such a way as to bring the greatest good to the country. To resist them is to resist the finer aspects of the nation's nobility and exceptionalism. If they do not get with it, as Barbara Bush warned, they will not be able to attract new immigrants to their party and they may find it difficult to win future elections.

The Content of an Immigration Reform Bill

What should be the real content of any immigration reform measure? To begin with, the Congress and the president should not settle for any bill that is piecemeal. It must be broad-based, comprehensive, progressive, fair and enforceable. The following should be essential elements of such a Bill.

The DREAM Act

The DREAM Act should be passed without delay. Having a large number of young people cowering in fear of being deported is not noble; it is un-American. I well remember the fear and anxiety in the voice of a young Haitian as she dreaded her approaching graduation from high school. Instead of looking at this signal event with hope and optimism she was distraught for graduation could very well have meant the end of her stay in America. Her anxiety dissipated when President Obama announced his initiative to no longer detain and deport undocumented young people like herself. They could now come out from under the shadows (and thousands did) with a chance at realizing their dreams in the country they had grown to love and call home.

These young people simply want to get on with their studies and their lives without having to look over their shoulders or jump each time they hear a knock on the door or see a policeman walk by. The great majority of them are not looking for handouts from government as they already know from observing their parents what it means to work hard. From very early in their lives they have been inoculated against the "entitlement" virus. It is important that the DREAM Act be made an integral part of any reform initiative or be passed independently as a matter of urgency. One can be sure that the president will continue to exercise executive authority over its provisions outside of Congress, but if it were to become settled law, it would give greater certainty, clarity and peace of mind to those that it is intended to help.

Pathway to Citizenship

It is also imperative that as part of any reform the status of the almost eleven million undocumented persons living in the country be regularized. Control and management of immigration has now become a national security matter even more than it has been prior to the terrorist attack on America. An open, porous border is a recipe for disaster. Efforts must be stepped up to reinforce security, especially on the southern border. There must be an end to the political games being played with this sensitive area of the nation's security. No effort should be spared in providing the necessary manpower and surveillance technology that are necessary in this effort. It is inconceivable to regularize the status of those here illegally before something fulsome and well meaning is done to secure the nation' borders. To do otherwise is tantamount to giving an open invitation to others to come into the country in expectation of reprieve.

To regularize the status of the undocumented should not to be equated with amnesty. This is a word that is repulsive to the Republican Party whenever the issue of immigration is being addressed. It figured prominently in the defeat of the Bush initiative. It is a highly emotive word and not one of endearment in the immigrant community. The emotionalism that attends the word often ignores the reality that many of those who are in the country illegally do not expect to be given a free pass. There is no overwhelming evidence to suggest that they are not willing to abide by even strict guidelines in order to become citizens. They will pay a price as long as there is the assurance that they will have the freedom to live their lives without fear or intimidation. Republican spokespersons have clearly placed the party on the wrong side of the debate on this issue by mischaracterizing a pathway to citizenship as amnesty. This kind of diatribe muddies the water as it conveys a lack of compassion and inclusivity, which are essential elements of any notion of American exceptionalism. Furthermore, it masks essential ingredients of the American spirit for fairness. It is not farfetched to suggest that such rhetoric is un-American. To demonstrate that they are for a meaningful and just reform of the system, Republicans would be well advised to tone down the rhetoric. They can begin by erasing the word "amnesty" from their vocabulary.

Employment Verification

It would seem obvious that verification of employees' status has to become an integral part of any immigration reform initiative in the future. Once people are placed on a path to citizenship, the government must vigorously enforce the laws against businesses that continue to employ undocumented workers. There has to be a zero tolerance approach to this matter. Fines and penalties must justify the gravity of the offence. Slaps on the wrist will not do. Part of the reason for the present predicament in the immigration process is the laxity of the federal government in enforcing the immigration laws. This laxity has given fillip to certain states such as Arizona to adopt an individual approach to the problem often in contravention of federal guidelines and violation of people's constitutional rights.. It is not helpful for individual states to go on a frolic of their own. We have seen the unintended consequences of this approach especially in the area of ethnic and racial profiling.

Work Visas

America trains the brightest minds in the world at its renowned universities, yet, at the end of their training, many graduates who would want to stay in the country, start businesses and generally contribute to the development of the economy, leave or otherwise remain in the country illegally. As undocumented persons they live in anxiety and fear of deportation. Sometimes the prospects of going back to their home country are not appealing. Any sensible immigration possible would roll out the welcome mat to such talent. It is what a dynamic and progressive country would do as such talent can only augment innovation and growth in the economy.

Also, a carefully worked out program to allow guest workers to come in on a quota system to fill jobs that Americans are not doing or are not willing to do should be considered. The agricultural sector especially would benefit from this initiative as well as workers in the information technology sector.

There is no doubt that signing a bill for comprehensive reform of the broken immigration system would be a major feather in the President's political cap. But comprehensive immigration reform has to be about more than a president burnishing his presidential legacy. Neither can it be about the reluctance of his political opponents to give him a major political victory. The immigration system is impatient of major reform and should not be the subject political gamesmanship. Shorn of its partisan, political characteristics, it is the moral thing to do. It is what is right and good for the country at this time. The present debate may be the last big chance that the country will have to get an immigration bill that will comprehensively reform the process well into the next decade and beyond.

Any attempt at reform must therefore be bold and should not merely tinker with the process or be characterized by a haphazard approach. A piecemeal approach will merely kick the can down the road. It should be clear that no future administration will be able to mount comprehensive reform that veers too far from what has been suggested in the Bush/Obama plans outlined above. There is a certain momentum that has been built up in the present debate. It would be a great disappointment if this momentum is sacrificed on the altars of political intransigence, for not only would the present problems not be solved, but they will continue to fester to the greater detriment of the country. No country that claims to be exceptional, diverse, pluralistic and inclusive can await the luxury of delay in this matter. Immigration is on an inevitable march to reform. Those who would want to hold it back in order to satisfy narrow interests and guarantee their own political longevity must know that they are on the wrong side of the debate. The people have had enough of the political pussyfooting and dithering on this matter. They will not be kind to those who continue to obstruct for the sake of obstructing or who allow petulance to become a humbug to the nation's progress. There must be a greater determination to climb the high moral ground to progress that immigration reform beckons.

Notes on Chapter Two

1. From "Electric Cord" Speech given by Abraham Lincoln on July 10, 1858, Chicago, Illinois; *The Collected Works of Abraham Lincoln, Vol. II*, ed. Roy P. Basler (New Brunswick, NJ: Rutgers University Press, 1953), 499-500.

2. President Ronald Reagan, farewell address to the nation, January 11, 1989.

3. Pew Research, *The Rise of Asian Americans*, updated edition, April 4, 2013

CHAPTER THREE

THE IMPERATIVE OF SOCIAL JUSTICE

Human progress is neither automatic nor inevitable... Every step toward the goal of justice requires sacrifice, suffering, and struggle; the tireless exertions and passionate concern of dedicated individuals- **(Martin Luther King, Jr.)**

What makes America exceptional are the bonds that hold us together; the belief that our destiny is shared; that this country only works when we accept certain obligations to another and future generations. **(President Barack Obama, Post-election Acceptance Speech, November 6, 2012).**

<<<<<<>>>>>>

The struggle for social justice is an unending one that has to be won incrementally with a great deal of perseverance and sacrifice. This is what Martin Luther King, Jr., that icon of the Civil Rights movement, recognized in the difficult fight to restore the dignity not only of the black person but of all oppressed peoples in the world. It is the lesson to be learnt from Mahatma Gandhi, in that martyr's long struggle against the British Raj in securing Indian independence. It is also the lesson to be learnt from the anguished and noble life of Nelson Mandela, that great South African icon and quintessential international citizen, in his struggle against apartheid in his native land. The cry for social justice is heard in all corners of the earth and it is no less so in the United States.

Social justice, properly understood, is not a mere abstract idea but goes to the very root of what makes for a civilized society. In the struggle against injustice King, Gandhi and Mandela well understood the strong humanistic traditions in which the principle was rooted. But their acquaintance with the term was not forged in philosophical debate or rhetoric, but in the harsh, practical realities of the injustice with which they and their oppressed brothers and sisters had to contend. It was forged out of the brutality of the mental and physical pain that were evident in beatings, imprisonments, and in isolation from family that attended the efforts for social change.

It is instructive to note that the three men referred to above have left a greater and more indelible footprint on the world stage than perhaps any other person in the twentieth, and so far, the twenty-first century. This insight is owed to a friend who brought it to my attention. It is further instructive, that the reason for their massive footprints and international stature as world citizens is that they were prepared to pay with their lives (which two did) for the principles they believed in. When the moment demanded of them horrendous sacrifice for the sake of their poor, oppressed, and marginalized fellow citizens, they rose to the occasion, thus satisfying that greater nobility in the human spirit that man indeed does not live by bread alone.

In the case of King, his view of social justice was fully grounded in the insistence that America, in giving legitimacy to institutionalized racism under the Jim Crow laws, had departed from the founding documents that gave sanctity to its existence. This was particularly important since these documents were grounded in the Judeo-Christian ethic which emphasized one's love for God and responsibility to one's fellowmen. It was the insistence that everyone had a right to be treated fairly; that each person's humanity was not a gift from men but from God, his Creator, which ought to be preserved, protected and defended. As Jefferson had brilliantly noted in the preamble to the Declaration of Independence, it was the business of government to protect and preserve these rights. When it failed to do so, as was the case in segregated

America under Jim Crow, citizens were guaranteed the freedom under the Constitution to vigorously protest and seek redress.

King and his followers chose the non-violent path to social change. This imbued the movement with the moral authority to challenge the principalities and powers of the status quo to bring about needed change. Society loses its legitimacy whenever people's rights are not preserved, or whenever the resources of the state are reserved for the benefit of a few at the expense of the many. This creates systemic inequities and structural distortions in the distribution of goods and services. These have to be dismantled and replaced with more humane systems.

This is what the struggle for social justice, properly understood, is about. It is within the context of these structural and systemic inequalities that the cry for social justice in America has become so palpable today. The Democratic Party has long been seen as the "social justice party" with the Republicans being consistently regarded as the party of the rich. This divide, as will be noted later, was very sharp in the last presidential elections. Part of the problem that the Republican Party faces and which it does not seem too willing to admit, and which it must admit and correct if it is to have a viable future, is the confusion in its camp as to what social justice is all about. It might therefore be helpful to remind ourselves what we are talking about when we use the term.

For the liberal wing of the political spectrum social justice means, among other things, the redistribution of resources to the poor, downtrodden and oppressed minorities in society. Their belief is that the government has a solemn obligation to help those in need and if helping them means moving resources from the rich and wealthy who can afford it, to the poor and dispossessed, then this ought to be done. Those who advocate this radical reorganization of society are usually left of the political spectrum and are often, though not exclusively, defenders of Democratic Party principles.

The conservative wing does not believe in the wholesale redistribution of resources from the wealthy to the poor. They believe that this undermines the work ethic; that people should work hard for what they have and should not be allowed to grow dependent on government for their every need. They particularly resent taxation that moves money from the rich to support government spending programs. Identified as being on the extreme right of the political spectrum, they believe in small government and individual initiative and ascribe minimum role to government while resenting its intrusion into people's lives. Conservative values largely favor the Republican Party.

There was a time in the 1960's and early 1970's when no one doubted what social justice meant. Then, the divide between the liberal and conservative camps was not as radicalized as it is today. The concept, undergirded by biblical principles, enjoyed a place of prominence in social discourse. But today, it has become sandwiched between liberal and conservative ideology to the extent that the use of the term has become very polarized between competing political ideologies. So deep has the polarization become that if you are an advocate for social justice, you are likely to be called a progressive, socialist or communist. This is why President Obama is caricatured as a socialist by conservatives.

> The history of evangelicalism in America is not one which has supported any vocal or passionate advocacy against institutionalized injustice.

Even the conservative evangelical wing of the church seems not to be too comfortable with the term social justice. Their discomfort with it as social progressivism is largely supported by the conservative press greatly represented by the *Fox News Network*. While evangelicals will do charitable deeds in tandem with what they believe to be their Christian witness demands, such as opening pantries, running soup kitchens or pandering to emaciated orphans in Africa, they will disavow any appeal to activism to challenge political and economic structures in society which breed unfairness and trample on the rights of others. The history of evangelicalism in America is not one which has supported any vocal or passionate advocacy against institutionalized injustice.

Their concern is not with a social gospel but with a privatized view of Christianity which pours scorn and derision on social activism. To propagate a social gospel which enshrines social protest or promotes reform or social change is to derogate from what they believe to be the true Gospel. Like many of their conservative counterparts, they believe social activism is rooted in socialism or Marxism and has no basis in the Christian gospel. This is so for social justice is viewed by the Christian Right as a redistribution of wealth from the rich to the poor members of society. They do not often see the discrepancies that are often conveyed in Republican budgets (as are represented, for example, in the Paul Ryan budget recommendations) which call for the gutting of social programs that are intended to benefit the poor while at the same time maintaining subsidies and tax loopholes that favor the rich. Is this reversed socialism? Is it redistribution only when benefits flow from the rich to the poor but sound economic policy when it goes in the other direction? History will record that the Bush tax cuts will constitute one of the most massive redistribution of wealth from the poor to the rich that has ever taken place in America. Until it was minimized in 2012, Bush's tax incentive for wealthy Americans was the longest running "crash program" for the rich that the country had experienced for a long time. This is one program that the Republican Party struggled in vain to make permanent.

With this kind of corporate welfare why should corporate America be worried about the work ethic? All that one has to do is move paper around in one gigantic game of paper chase, or invest in hedge funds or questionable securities. After all, if there is failure the Federal Reserve will come to the rescue. Is this the reason why corporate America is sitting on trillions of dollars instead of deploying that formidable resource in creating new jobs in an anemic job market?. In the mind of the conservative right, both in politics and religion, it would appear that the work ethic is destroyed only when the poor get help from government, not when the rich do. The rich can sit on their high pile of capital without deploying it productively to aid the growth of the economy. Yet they are given substantial tax breaks under the guise that they will create jobs. To some in the conservative right, this is okay for after all the rich, in the words of F. Scott Fitzgerald, are different from you and me; or in the infamous words of Leona Hemsley, only the little people pay taxes. It is true that evangelicals, like liberals, stress the necessity of hard work as the way to prosperity, but there seems to be a moral disconnect in the mind of the evangelical which refuses to recognize that people who are genuinely in need ought to be helped.

What is Social Justice?

Before the term was bastardized by the conservative press as social progressivism, socialism or even communism, the term social justice had an important pedigree in social liberal discourse in America and the West in general. What then is social justice or justice as the Bible understands it? Without being too technical, seen in purely sociological terms "social" refers to people living together in organized communities. The largest grouping of people within a defined geographical border is referred to as a nation which is in turn composed of subsets of groups within it. The word "social" would suggest that there is a certain level of cohesion and interaction that hold these groups and ultimately the nation together; that they are defined by particular cultural values and are influenced by a common set of goals to be achieved. It is assumed that the members will work together to accomplish these goals. If the goals are common to the community or nation, then it is assumed that the resources in the community will be used to fulfill the common good for all.

The fulfillment of the common good is a function of a just, humane and orderly society. *TheOxford Dictionary* defines justice as "just behavior or treatment or the quality of being fair and reasonable." *The American Heritage Dictionary* sees it as the upholding of what is just and conforming to moral rightness in action or attitude. These definitions take into account two basic aspects with which social justice ought to be concerned- retributive or remedial justice and distributive justice.

Retributive or Remedial Justice
This deals with the rules governing civil and criminal proceedings and sanctions that are meted out for illegal or inappropriate behavior. The essential concern here is whether society is organized to give people a fair chance to participate in the political and legal system and whether particular groups in society bear disproportionate burdens by how laws are executed and sanctions prescribed. For example, national statistics bear out that on a per capita basis more blacks are incarcerated in America than their white counterparts for drugs and other crimes. Also, at any given time, there are more blacks on death row in America than any other racial group.

In the context of retributive or remedial justice, there are three matters that should be of tremendous concern to Americans who are concerned about social justice.

1. The Burgeoning Prison Industrial Complex
The privatization of prisons in many states has raised alarm at what is being described as the prison industrial complex where prisoners are "warehoused" for commercial gain. One of these "warehouses" which brands itself as "America's leader in partnership corrections" is the Corrections Corporation of America (CCA). In its 2012 annual report, it positioned itself as the nation's largest owner of partnership correctional facilities and leading corrections management provider to federal, state and local governmental agencies. The 2012 report stated that it operated over 67 facilities with design capacity for close to 100,000 beds in 20 states and the District of Columbia.

In its 2012 letter to shareholders, CCA expressed great pleasure that the company posted record revenues for the year due mainly to new contracts, higher compensated populations (a euphemism for a growing inmate population) and growth in average per diem rates. In other words, CCA has seen spectacular growth since its founding 30 years ago. Its business model for 2013 would see the corporation re-configured into a fully functioning Real Estate Investment Trust (REIT). REITs do not pay income tax as long as their taxable earnings are distributed to shareholders as dividends. Thus, the reduction of its tax liability will enable CCA, by its own admission, to "contribute to our double digit growth in net income and enable us to increase the regular quarterly dividend to our investors by *165% in 2013*."[1] (italics mine). Who would want to see the death of this cash cow? What is shown up in this report is precisely what is to be feared by the burgeoning profitability of this industry. Such obscene profit is set against the background of the reality that the United States has the world's highest rate of incarceration with close to 2.5 million people behind bars. Blacks and Hispanics are disproportionately incarcerated when compared to their white cohorts. Incarceration is due mainly to rising illegal immigration and the failed and elusive war on drugs.

The private prison industry, of which CCA is the industry leader, places a great deal of emphasis on the expansion of bed capacity to meet expected demands. The Justice Policy Institute, a Washington-based think-tank dedicated to reducing the nation's reliance on incarceration, identifies three strategies that are employed by CCA and other players in the industry in their drive to enhance and expand business. They influence public policy on incarceration by lobbying, make direct contributions to state and federal politicians in both parties and network relentlessly. The bulk of the effort is expended on lobbying and campaign finance contributions with Republicans getting the lion's share of these contributions.

One is not saying that privatizing prisons is wrong. In fact, private sector participation can bring important synergies to relieving the strain on state and federal authorities in the management of prisons. But concern must be raised for a system that seems to be more concerned about making profit from the incarceration of people than their rehabilitation. Of course, the industry will retort that it does not create prison populations but merely manage what is sent to them. It will also argue, as it has done, that it is engaged in rehabilitation which reduces the rates of recidivism. But one has to question what lies behind its intense lobbying of politicians to influence policy ostensibly to keep these prisons filled; to ensure that laws are enacted to guarantee a gradual "pipeline" of human beings to these facilities.

Also, the question must be asked as to how robust is the industry about rehabilitation. How much of its resources go to that effort compared to what is spent on building new facilities and expanding bed capacity? The industry closely resembles a Ponzi scheme as it thrives on numbers that are added to these prison facilities daily. A reduced prison population is not good for business. There can be no doubt that the private prison industry has a vested interest in keeping these facilities humming. This inevitably leads to the increase of prison populations not to their decrease. Anyone concerned about social justice would want to be concerned about the growth of this industry, whether in the private or public sector. One wonders where the thinking of the church is on these matters.

2. The Meltdown of the Financial Sector in 2008

Remedial justice should also be concerned with the Meltdown of the Financial Sector which precipitated the 2008 recession. What diligence was exercised by the regulators to prevent the meltdown? Were the necessary legal mechanisms in place to prevent it? If people were criminally culpable what sanctions were or will be meted out to the perpetrators of this criminal activity? What mechanisms will be put in place to prevent a recurrence of this sort of thing in the future? These questions are not easily answered but any properly functioning legal system ought to be cognizant of them. It is only in recent times that the Department of Justice has awoken to the need to pursue the big banks and hold them accountable for their role in fraudulent practices in the mortgage industry which precipitated the meltdown. But the overwhelming national sentiment is that enough is not being done to punish those who by their greed hurt many and hounded some to early graves. Many have lost faith in the justice system for they believe it is rigged and stacked against the poor and helpless.

3. Guantanamo Bay: America's Gulag

The terrorist detention camp at Guantanamo Bay, Cuba, was established by the Bush Administration as a holding place for enemy combatants who were captured in places like Afghanistan and Iraq in the ongoing fight against Al Qaeda and its affiliates. In 2008, as a presidential candidate, President Obama campaigned on a platform to close the camp in his first term in office. Soon after his election he moved speedily to release 67 detainees who were cleared to be returned to other countries. But he did not reckon with the opposition he would have received from Congress, even from members of the Democratic Party. It was not long after the transfers began that a democratically controlled Congress imposed restrictions on any further transfer of detainees or any attempt to move them to the US mainland.

At a press conference at the White House on May 1, 2013, the president expressed disgust, outrage and frustration at the continuing obscenity that the camp had become. In a later speech on national security at the National Defense University, he affirmed his frustration that the camp has remained open. Serious questions have been raised about the constitutionality of the camp, but the president now had greater moral clarity that it did not represent the values of a free America; that it had become a symbol unworthy of the best tenets of social justice.

This unworthy state of affairs of detaining people indefinitely without trial has persisted to the extent that the remaining detainees, some of whom have already been cleared for transfer, went on a hunger strike to protest their unjust and unconscionable suspension in purgatory. The administration at GITMO, as the camp is called, force fed these inmates to keep them alive. It is not clear to what end they are being kept alive as there is no coherent policy as to whether the camp will be closed or retained as a "warehouse" for those who have not even been tried and proven to have committed crimes against America. This state of affairs is untenable and is in fact a blot on America's standing as a just nation.

The President is right: GITMO does not represent the best values of the American people. It is not within the nation's value system to lock people up and as it were forget about them. Such behavior is reminiscent of what the Russians did in the Cold War era in detaining their own citizens in horrible concentration camps so well documented by Alexander Solzhenitsyn in his book *The Gulag Archipelago*. We may not be detaining our own citizens at GITMO, but every well thinking American should be outraged at this horrible rape of people's humanity. GITMO has fast become America's gulag. What is happening there would not be allowed on the US mainland. This perhaps explains why politicians on both sides of the political fence strenuously resist them being taken to the American mainland. Some people seem to think that as long as we keep the detainees there we will not have to deal with them in the USA.

Largely in silence, this obscenity has been allowed to persist because the principles of natural and social justice have been abandoned. The values of fairness and respect for the dignity of persons that have informed the Judeo-Christian founding of America no longer seem relevant in the face of this atrocity. In the eyes of some, these detainees are already guilty and are deserving of the inhumane treatment that is being meted out to them. But GITMO is un-American in every way. Social justice demands its closure however hard this may be for some to accept. As the president rightly acknowledged, history will cast a harsh judgment on America for GITMO and those who fail to end it. History might have already rendered its verdict.

Distributive Justice

Distributive justice addresses how society is organized to ensure that people share in the burdens and benefits of maintaining a viable society. It deals with the structural impediments which militate against people being able to enjoy certain benefits that are due to them. Distributive justice would be concerned with the question as to whether benefits are fairly distributed, not only within particular classes or races, but across the broad spectrum of society. This is a concern that will become more important in the years ahead as the society becomes more diversified among ethnic groups and as demographic changes tug at the cords of social cohesion. The provision of safety nets for the weakest will increasingly become more obvious but how this is attended to will be a matter of great conjecture.

Distributive justice is not only concerned with how benefits are distributed but who bears the burden for the orderly distribution of these benefits. This is where the rub is for there is never a free lunch; someone has to pay. Social benefits have to be paid for by taxpayers and there is an overwhelming consensus that American taxpayers are already overburdened. The debate is still raging as to whether the big entitlement programs of government are sustainable. Will taxes have to be raised to pay for them and if so who should be called upon to bear the greater share? Is it time to reform these programs, to ensure a more efficient distribution of benefits and that benefits go only to those for whom they are intended?

These are difficult questions to answer as can be seen from the acrimony that has developed on both sides of the debate. However well-intentioned one may be, the proper allocation of a nation's resources will never be done to everyone's satisfaction. No society has a clear template as to who should reap the most benefits or bear the most burdens for society's good. These matters are settled by negotiation and compromise. Distributive justice would be concerned that in such negotiations it is not a matter of who wins or who loses but whether the common good of the society is served.

And the common good must be fundamentally related to what makes for a healthy and prosperous society. What should be quite clear is that the concentration of benefits in the hands of a few at the expense of the impoverishment of the many will not bode well for society's health. Neither will social cohesion be helped by asking the few to bear the burdens of the many. Properly understood, the biblical insistence on social justice can point to that middle ground or proper balance that has to be struck. In fact, throughout the nation's history, insistence on this principle has been the glue that has held society together in terms of the appeal to fundamental fairness in the way society is organized for the greater good.

It has meant the difference between a path to chaos and a path to community, and is an essential part of what America is as an exceptional nation. Sadly, this reality is being lost in the political chatter of the day even among the churches that should be the purveyors of this essential principle. So there is an urgent need to regain and reassert the biblical principle of social justice and re-establish its rightful place in the nation's public discourse. But given the confusion about social justice in the media, it may be helpful to remind ourselves what this biblical principle is about. To a brief description of this we now turn.

The Biblical Principle of Social Justice
Whatever may be the definition of social justice by the media or other areas of secular society it is important that the church understands what social justice is and how this relates to its mission in the world. For some Christians social justice means just being kind and neighborly to people. It means giving to a worthy cause especially when the conscience is seared by ugly images of starving children in Africa. For others it means showing pity for the suffering person, like the priest and Levite in the story of the Good Samaritan, but never demonstrating the compassion of the Samaritan or putting one's life at risk, or becoming truly engaged in human suffering.

Still, for others, social justice is all that social activism represents. It is the social gospel in action. It has nothing to do with a privatized view of religion but one which fully engages the structures of oppression and injustice to bring about radical change in the human situation. This is pretty much how Dr. Martin Luther King saw it. It is to see Jesus not just as the "gentle Jesus meek and mild" of one's Sunday school experience, but as the "political Christ" who was not afraid to challenge the political and religious authorities of His day with the urgent demands of the Kingdom of God.

In his long struggle for social justice, King and the leaders of the Civil Rights movement well understood the need to be charitable and loving to one's neighbor. But he also knew that an unjust society cannot be changed by wishful thinking or simply by just being charitable to one's neighbor, or by an appeal to one's more angelic nature. He knew from the biblical perspective that social justice cuts deeper than that and makes a more urgent demand on the Christian than mere charity would allow.

Yet, today, it would appear that most Christians seem satisfied with the belief that they are carrying out the demands of building a just and equitable society by their righteous deeds of charity. It would appear that not many Christians would be convinced that joining a march on Wall Street to protest the greed that led to the financial meltdown, the attendant suffering of many in home foreclosures and loss of jobs, and the growing income inequality in the society are issues that Christians should be involved with. For many on the Christian Right, it is sufficient to carry out one's Christian duty by simply writing a check to the Red Cross, but marching for justice and equity is what socialists do. It is a Michael Moore thing, or what the loony left does, but not something that Christians should be doing. There is a very serious disconnect in the minds of many Christians which prevents them from understanding that the problems of injustice in society are often of a systemic and structural nature and that they are hard to solve outside of a robust activism for change. This lack of understanding could perhaps explain why many Christians do not get involved, or why they see charitable deeds as an excuse not to be radically involved to bring about the needed change.

Jefferson and the Immorality of Slavery

The needed change, certainly the essential appeal of social justice, is that every person be treated as a person and not a thing or a mere cog in a machine that can be exploited for profit. "Justice," wrote Tillich, "is always violated if men are dealt with as if they were things."[2] The ultimate tragedy of slavery was the perpetuation of the belief that slaves were not human beings but mere chattel or things. This gave justification to the brutality that was meted out to them. The owners were able to set up a firewall between their conscious acts of brutality and any suggestion from their conscience that they were doing wrong; that the "chattel" they were treating with such brutality were living, breathing human beings like themselves.

With this firewall firmly established in their consciousness, they could do with their slaves as they wished. Human laws aided and abetted their brutality and there was hardly any space left for the moral law to cause even a pause in their brutality. The fact that many of these slave owners were members of the church did nothing to blunt their desire to subdue and conquer the rebellious chattel. There was nothing about which their conscience had to be afraid since that had already been dulled by the thinking that the slaves were not humans. It was the slave's utility value that was important, not their intrinsic worth, which any definition of them as human beings would have required. The fact that some members of the clergy owned slaves gives credence to the extent to which conscience was dulled to serve a commercial principle.

Without this dulling of conscience it would be difficult for a planter not to face the reality that the child that was born to him as a result of an affair with a slave was his and was a human being like himself. There could now be no distinction between the white child and the colored other than the obvious color of the skin. But they were both human! This is the humanity that was defined in that immortal preamble to the Declaration of Independence penned by Jefferson who himself owned slaves and impregnated at least one slave on his estate. If it had dawned on him that slaves were included in that glorious declaration that ***all*** men are created **equal** and that they were endowed by their Creator (not by the legislature, the judiciary or any other man-made system) with **unalienable** rights, would the Declaration have undergone considerable editing? Since slaves were not defined as humans, it was easy to perpetuate the contradiction contained in their possession and denigration while producing a lofty, moral document that spoke to the essential freedom and intrinsic worth of man.

The issue here is not whether men like Jefferson treated their slaves humanely, but that they themselves owned slaves. To own a slave was itself an inhumane act since it was to support a system that degraded the value of human life. There is no sense of humanity in a system that degrades people's self worth. Under slave conditions there was no happiness to be pursued by a slave as long as he was tied to the plantation. Where there is no liberty there can be no pursuit of happiness.

Despite Jefferson's flaws and his mistakes in the slave trade, he was right to assert the equality of all people. Not only is this concept asserted in the

> *Where there is no liberty there can be no pursuit of happiness.*

biblical creation narrative, but it forms a basic foundation of social justice as it speaks to the intrinsic worth of every human being. If every human being is considered equal in the sight of God, having been implanted with his image (the Imago Dei), then there should be no room for the exploitation of one person by another. It is particularly detestable to do this on the basis of a person's skin color. This explains why racism is such a pernicious and damnable system and why, frankly, many Americans are not comfortable talking about it and would simply wish it to go away. But almost daily we are reminded of how deeply embedded racism is in the nation's psyche. Incidents such as the white Mississippi teens who killed a black man (Craig Anderson, 49) simply because they wanted to find a black man to kill or James Byrd who was dragged to death in Texas by three white men, demonstrate that racism is alive in America. These incidents may be the more grotesque manifestations of racism, but more insidious and pernicious is the institutionalized racism that continues to deny the poor and marginalized the fundamental underpinnings of social justice. They indicate why as a society there is the urgent need for a frank dialogue about race relations.

It is not my intention to go into a full scale analysis of the biblical perspective on social justice. Even a cursory reading of the Old and New Testaments will reveal an irrefutable truth: justice, the need to do right by one's fellow men, is a cardinal virtue that goes to the very nature of who God is. The biblical narrative indicates that God takes a special interest in the poor, a principle which is often referred to in Christian theology as the option for the poor. This interest is taken precisely because the poor are vulnerable, are easily exploited by the rich and often have no one to speak for them or to plead their cause. They can be easily trampled on by the wealthy who use their wealth to influence or wield tremendous political power against them in the society. There is a particular concern demonstrated for widows and orphans. Without husbands to defend them, the widow was often left to the merciless exploitation of men. Without parents or guardians, orphans were left to roam the streets. They were often beaten or sold into slavery.

The Work of the Eighth Century Prophets
It is in the work of the eighth century prophets in Israel that this preferential option for the poor was more robustly expressed. This prophetic period seemed to have been of particular importance to Martin Luther King. In his sermons and speeches he seemed to have drawn a great deal of inspiration and strength from these prophets, especially Amos and Micah. For him, these were not mere ancient texts which were relevant for people at a particular time, but which stood for all time as representing the mind of God against injustice of any kind. Today the work of these prophets rings with refreshing relevance and

can help to reinvigorate the church in standing up for social justice. It will be helpful that we rediscover them.

In doing so it is useful to look at the socio-economic and religious background of this period in Israel's history. The biblical material for this period is contained in the historical books of 2 Kings 14: 3-17 and 2 Chronicles 25-28 and in the prophetic work of Isaiah, Amos, Jonah, Hosea and Micah. The period was one of unprecedented prosperity and military expansion in both the Northern (Israel) and Southern (Judah) kingdoms. This prosperity was largely seen in the long reign of King Jeroboam 11 (786-746 B.C.) in the south. The relative prosperity that both states enjoyed was largely the result of the absence of military conflict which aided a rapid expansion of trade between the two kingdoms. With this rapid economic growth many in the ruling and commercial classes became wealthy. They lived extravagant lifestyles consistent with their wealth. But their lifestyle was predicated on oppressive credit conditions meted out to the lower classes and blatant commercial exploitation of the weak.

There are two basic elements that defined the prophetic outrage against existing conditions in both states.

a. **The denunciation of injustice**. The growth of the wealthy class sharpened the distinction between the "haves" and the "have-nots." Amos was particularly offended by the way in which the poor was taxed and exploited to pay for the excesses of the rich (Amos 5: 11-13). The rich failed to see that privilege carried with it responsibility. The absence of a social and ethical construct led to great harm being done especially to the poorer and more vulnerable members of society.

It is not difficult to see a parallel in America today especially since the financial meltdown on Wall Street. The guardians of the financial sector got filthily rich from the securitization of junk mortgages which eventually poisoned the entire financial system. This imposed great hardships on many families as job losses and foreclosures became the order of the day. Despite clever maneuvering by the Federal Reserve through a dubious mechanism called quantitative easing (QE), people continue to suffer from the less than robust growth in the economy. What is clear is that retirees who have saved for the rainy day have seen their income diminish by a protracted low return on their savings. Yet, the stock market has been buoyant, thanks to the intervention of the Federal Reserve.

There may be some merit to the Federal Reserve policy, but one of the horrible results of it is the savaging of the middle class, as increasing members, by dint of falling incomes or unemployment, are not able to participate in the stock market or in the wider economy. One does not have to be an economist to know that the economy is terribly skewed and heavily weighted against the poor and the shrinking middle class. Neither is it difficult to see that the economy is only benefiting the rich and well heeled, the top 10 percent, including the big banks that have truly now become too big to fail. What has become obvious in the global economic crisis as it has played out in America, is the blatant disregard for the neighbor occasioned by the toxicity of greed.

There is hardly anything to suggest that the moral sensibilities of the powerful players on Wall Street have been offended by what is happening to the middle class and the poorest in the society. Indeed, in the aftermath of the financial meltdown, many on Wall

> *There has never been a social or economic system, however corrupt, that does not have its defenders and protectors.*

Street, with their willing accomplices in the Congress, have opposed any attempt at regulation which would ensure that this travesty is never again visited upon the country. The Republican Party is fully committed to repeal the Dodd-Frank legislation (the *Dodd-Frank Wall Street Reform and Consumer Protection Act*) which is intended to regulate the financial sector, protect consumers and restrain the greedy in their thrust for profits at all costs. But there has never been a social or economic system, however corrupt, that does not have its defenders and protectors. There are those who benefit handsomely from this arrangement and have no wish for the party to stop. But while they are having a grand time people are suffering and even dying.

What is particularly sad is that those who are elected and given power to take care of the people's business are often the ones who corruptly and unethically use their power to further the interests of the rich and powerful. In recent times the Republican Party has been identified as the party that has stood at the center of this unconscionable support of the strong and powerful against the weak. Their opposition to continued unemployment insurance support for those that need it, coupled with their avowed desire to cut food stamp benefits to poor families, are particularly horrendous. This cannot be good for the long term health of the society for at some point the bonds of social cohesion will become severely strained and the unintended consequences of civil disobedience, and even violence, may be the result.

The least that the church can do in situations like these is to stand on the side of justice. Like the prophets of old it cannot stand idly by without voicing concern that the richest banking and financial corporations are bailed out by taxpayers only for them to expel people from their homes, sometimes through fraudulent foreclosure procedures. The church that follows the mandate of Jesus should have a leadership role in denouncing the injustice that is being meted out to many because of the actions of a few. It is appalling that in this financial mess no one has been found legally accountable for what has taken place. The wrist of a few banks have been slapped as if they were just mere naughty boys or miscreants who took some cookie from a jar; not as highway robbers who brought the system into disrepute and by doing so ruined the lives of many. Where is the prophetic voice of the church in all this? Where is the sense of outrage and the action to support that outrage?

b. **The corruption of worship**. In eighth century Israel, unprecedented prosperity characterized by abdication of moral responsibility inevitably led to a corruption of worship. Isaiah was particularly strident in the observation of what he saw as the disjunction between the injustices meted out to the poor and needy and the puerile attempt at worshiping God. For him and the other prophets, there was a direct correlation between worship and how others were treated. It was not acceptable that one could treat others unjustly or conduct corrupt business practices that hurt others and then kneel in praise of God with the belief that all was well. For the prophets this was rank hypocrisy and they called attention to it. Not only were such sacrifices hypocritical but they were in fact an offence to God (Isaiah 1: 13-15). What was required was repentance, a desire to seek justice, end oppression, defend the fatherless and plead the case of the widow (Isaiah 1: 16-17).Amos was equally scathing in his denunciation of the hypocritical attempts of the rich at worship (Amos 5: 21-23). What the Lord required was for justice to flow like water and righteousness like a mighty stream (Amos 5:24).

In the celebrated chapter 58 of Isaiah, there is a true fast (worship) that the Lord requires. It is to loosen the bonds of injustice, to lift the heavy burdens, to undo the yoke of bondage and to set the oppressed free (58:6). It is to share one's bread with the hungry; to provide shelter for the poor that have been cast out and to clothe the naked (58: 7). It is not seen in the exploitation of the laborer (58:3) or in the show of might by exhibiting the fist of wickedness (58:4). The fast that the Lord requires is best seen when the proper relationship between conduct (one's lifestyle) and worship is recognized. This is when true freedom will become a reality. For it is only as the yoke is taken away, wickedness no longer spoken and love extended to the hungry that the liberality of God's abundance will flow and society repaired and restored (58: 11-12).

The corruption of worship against which the prophets warned paved the way for the easy infiltration of idolatry and apostasy in the society. Without a moral compass to guide them it was not difficult for many to turn to the worship of other gods. Baal worship and the insertion of Canaanite fertility cults in the nation supplanted reverence for Yahweh.

Apostasy often becomes the first cousin of unprecedented prosperity. This tends to be the case whether in the life of a nation or that of an individual. Idol worship or the worship of self in the celebration of one's importance becomes the definitive mark of a society drunk on apostasy; that exchanges the truth for a lie, or which values profit above human need. The idolatrous indulgence of Israelite society no doubt lent legitimacy to the exploitation of the weak. It led to the weakening of the moral fiber of the nation and to its ultimate demise at the hands of the Babylonians. Is this where we are in America today?

The Challenge of Social Justice for the Church Today

One cannot be aware of the work of the eighth century prophets and feel their passion for justice without having a keen sense of how strikingly relevant their work is for the church today. In the atomized society in which we live, there is much in the work of the prophets to inspire the church's struggle against injustice. Yet, in the face of a growing consensus that there is a widening gap between the rich and the poor in America, the church seems to have grown strangely silent. In a recent report, the Pew Research Center stated that the median wealth of white households is 20 times that of blacks.[3] These are the worst ratios since government started publishing such data. This is directly related to the collapse of the housing market followed by the recession, but such disparities have been building up before the recession struck. Black families are losing their homes to foreclosure at a much faster pace than their white counterparts. Black median wealth fell by 66 percent, compared to Hispanic households at 53 percent and whites at 16 percent.

In a provocative and penetrating article in the *Vanity Fair* magazine, Joseph Stiglitz of Columbia University and Nobel Laureate in economics, noted that the upper one percent of Americans are taking in about a quarter of the nation's income every year and that they control 40 percent of the nation's wealth.[4] He argues that this state of affairs persists because this is how the wealthy want it to be. This group opposes any increase in taxes and favor lowering rates on capital gains. They exploit loopholes in the tax code which favor them and pay little or no income tax. They oppose any form of regulation-whether environmental and economic. Stiglitz argues that much of the inequality is due to the manipulation of the financial system, enabled by changes in the rules that have been bought and paid for by the financial industry itself.

What was clear in the collapse of Lehman Brothers and the 2008 financial crisis was how detached corporate America was from the cares and concerns of ordinary Americans. There is no indication that much has changed in this regard. What has become more obvious is that the biggest banks have grown bigger. There has to be something fundamentally wrong, even immoral, with an arrangement that allows big corporations to put people out of their homes, keep these homes locked up indefinitely, and then allow them to become dilapidated thus compromising the value of the properties of other homeowners in the area. The truth is that the big banks have become a net contributor to homelessness, yet they are allowed to profit obscenely from special bailouts and other incentives from government.

Also, there has to be something wrong with a policy that bails out big banks, some of which did not require a bailout, and which allows these institutions to withhold loans to small businesses that can barely survive without credit. Never mind that these businesses will not be able to re-tool or re-hire the frustrated hordes of the unemployed who became victims of Wall Street greed. And this after these banks benefitted from generous concessionary loans from the Federal Reserve and when it should have been clear to the regulatory authorities that such easy money was still being pumped into risky investments that caused the collapse in the first place. No wonder these institutions, with the uncompromisingly petulant help of the Republicans, are resisting strongly any attempt by the federal authorities to regulate them.

These issues have serious social justice implications as they breed structural inequalities in the society which may build social tensions that will hurt people at fundamental levels of their lives. But these are not issues about which large segments of the church seem to be concerned.

They are more concerned about "saving souls" without understanding the extent to which people's souls are being degraded by these social inequalities. Neither are they mindful of how these issues affect members of their churches, many of whom are hardly making it while the rich use their privileged positions to extract more benefits from the largesse of government. Those who are mindful of their prophetic call subject themselves to prophetic self-criticism while speaking on behalf of the poor and victimized. They are often vilified and dismissed as progressives, socialists or even communists.

Why is the church so silent in the face of these and other atrocities that are being meted out to the weakest and more vulnerable members of society? Where is the moral outrage and consequent social protest that once defined the church's response to issues of injustice? The church often speaks platitudes in a vacuum with a kind of superficiality that does not comport with where people are at the cutting edge of their suffering. Absent is a sense of prophetic self-criticism. While bigger churches and mega-ministries have been built, the church's prophetic critique of society and of itself has shrunken. Many

> While bigger churches and mega-ministries have been built, the church's prophetic critique of society and of itself has shrunken.

in the church have been consumed with an "edifice complex" and have fallen into the trap of defining success in worldly terms. The bigger the buildings, the larger the quantity of people who attend them, and the more affluent the lifestyle of the pastor, the more content people become that those who lead are carrying out the mandates of the gospel. Thus a great deal of pulpit time in many mega-churches is devoted to preaching a prosperity gospel which is intended to keep people happy. The sad reality is that much of this preaching is far removed from the practicality of the lives of those who listen to these messages.

Part of the reason that the church has grown silent has to do with its politicization. The church is more divided today politically than it has ever been in recent memory. The real divisions began with the ascendancy of the evangelical right with Jerry Falwell's Moral Majority movement and the formation of the Christian Coalition. Although these groups have largely faded in their influence and significance, there was a time when they exercised tremendous influence over Republican politics. Whatever entrenched influence the Evangelicals have over the Republican Party is largely attributable to the seminal work done by these groups in their heyday. They became a force to be reckoned with on conservative issues such as abortion, constitutional right to bear arms, homosexuality and small and limited government, to name a few. Even now, there is hardly a Republican presidential candidate that can become president without the blessings of the so-called religious right.

What might be described as the religious left or the liberal wing of the church is nothing to match the influence and political clout of the religious right. They neither have the monetary power or the overwhelming numbers of the evangelicals. Fringe liberal groups are out-organized and out-financed by evangelical Christians. Evangelicals give heavily to conservative causes and are likely to be more active in getting their views known and enlisting public sympathy for their positions on various issues. Not so liberal Christians who tend to be more cerebral or philosophical in their support of particular issues.

But whatever their separate postures the political lines of demarcation are clearly marked. The net result has been a greater intrusion of secular thinking on the agenda of the church. The intrusion of the homosexual agenda on the Episcopal, Lutheran and Presbyterian churches is a case in point. So too has been the thinking of large sections of evangelical Christianity with regard to social justice highlighted earlier. What is regrettable is that the Christian scriptures or long standing traditions that were based on the Christian scriptures, no longer seem to be what determines what the church should think or how it should act on particular issues. In matters of public policy, the views of

81

Bill O'Reilly, Rush Limbaugh, Sean Hannity and to some extent, Glenn Beck, are more likely to be listened to in the shaping of evangelical political consensus than those of leading evangelical pastors.

There can be no doubt that the division of the church into liberal and conservative camps has hurt the mission of the church. These divisions and their attendant disunity have led to widespread confusion and a diminution of the moral strength of the church. The loss of this moral strength is not only evident in America but is clearly seen in other Western societies. The number of atheists in America has doubled over the past decade. Many young people have lost faith in what they see as the moral ambivalence in the church and the downright hypocrisy in moral leadership that is offered by prominent leaders within it. The pedophile scandal in the Roman Catholic Church has added to the disillusionment of youth.

In Europe, the situation is even worse than in America. The secularization of Europe has picked up momentum over the past twenty years. Many now speak of a de-Christianized or post-Christian Europe as Christianity has been in full retreat in some countries. Like nature, religion abhors a vacuum, and so the space is being gladly filled by the advancing Muslims on the one hand, and atheistic philosophy on the other. There is a quip that Christianity has been so badly degraded in England that Anglican clergymen are more keepers of aquariums than fishers of men. Dwindling attendance in some of the big cathedrals tells the tale of this declining Christianity quite well. The average Sunday attendance in mainline churches in Europe and certainly in the Episcopal Church in America has fallen precipitously.

> *Where there is a fusion of politics and religion there is a tendency toward dictatorship and tyranny.*

One is not making an argument for a theocratic state. History bears testimony to the tragic consequences that flow out of arrangements in which human laws are made subservient to divine laws in order to preserve a political status quo. Where there is a fusion of politics and religion there is a tendency toward dictatorship and tyranny. Dean Inge, once the Dean of St. Paul's cathedral in England, presciently warned that the church that becomes married to the spirit of the age will become a widow in the next. Europe is witnessing the manifestation of Inge's prophetic statement. As far as his metaphor will allow, the American church is in serious marital crisis.

Jesus' Prophetic Mandate

It might not be enough, but the church may regain some respectability by at least re-discovering where it ought to be on the matter of social justice. To this end, it might be useful to end this section with a brief reminder of Jesus' understanding of His mandate as He began His ministry in Galilee. According to Luke's account, Jesus returned to Galilee filled with the power of the Spirit. He went into the synagogue at Nazareth and read from the book of the prophet Isaiah (49: 8, 9; 61: 1, 2). He then declared to His audience that what they had heard was being fulfilled in Him. This tremendous and for some, scandalous claim, stirred up great anger among some in the audience. They could not reconcile Mary's "little" boy and Joseph's carpentry apprentice with what they saw to be Jesus' claim to be the Messiah, the Anointed One, who could fulfill this prophecy. This was blasphemy of the highest order. No one so good could come out of Nazareth.

Their anger was perhaps stirred not only by Jesus' purported claim to be the Anointed one, but by the content of what was being claimed. What was that claim?

- a. He was anointed to preach the gospel to the poor.
- b. He was sent to heal the brokenhearted, to proclaim liberty to the captives, the recovery of sight to the blind and to set at liberty the oppressed.
- c. He was sent to proclaim the acceptable year of the Lord.

This was revolutionary language and some might have been hearing it for the first time. When Jesus claimed that these words pointed to himself they were forced to look at them in a different way. But Jesus was standing in the tradition of the Old Testament prophets when He declared God's preferential option for the poor. This is not to say that God does not care for the rich for he does have a concern for them.But the poor and oppressed do not have the many options that are open to the rich. Someone has to speak on their behalf. There has perhaps never been a time in the history of modern America when the voice of the church ought to be heard against the injustice being meted out to the poor and the weak. Its silence in this regard is deafening.

The Media Distortion of Social Justice

The understanding of social justice that has infused American social and political thought is derived ultimately from the strong Judeo-Christian ethic which forms the bedrock of the nation's founding. Much of the media discourse on social justice tends to distort the biblical perspective outlined above. Much of this distortion is to be seen in the work of some media practitioners, largely from the right, who equate social justice with a progressive, socialist agenda. It is therefore necessary to challenge this distortion as a large section of the Christian community has bought into it. This has only served to exacerbate the polarization of the church into distinct ideological camps. It reflects the extent to which the church has become wedded to the spirit of the age.

Like others in the society, the views of many Christians are likely to be shaped by what they hear or see in the press than what they hear from the pulpit. In the area of social justice, the situation is made worse when you consider that social justice themes with their strong biblical underpinning are hardly being heard today from the pulpits of our churches. There is certain gullibility on the conservative side to accept as gospel the pronouncements of a Rush Limbaugh or a Bill O'Reilly. On the liberal side minds are more likely to be influenced by the purveyors of political punditry at MSNBC such as Rachel Maddow, Ed Shultz or Chris Matthews.

Bill O'Reilly and Glenn Beck

In my view, Bill O'Reilly and Glenn Beck are the two media personalities who have done the most to distort what social justice is about. Since leaving *Fox News* Beck's role has diminished in this respect, but his views have helped to influence the confusion of social justice with socialism. On their respective shows they have made some of the most glaring distortions of the social justice theme. O'Reilly has built up an impressive following over the years. His *The O'Reilly Factor* continues to be the number one show on cable television. He is widely listened to and has a big following among conservatives and evangelical Christians. With this significant following the host of the program has a responsibility to ensure that what is transmitted about any subject is factual. I believe that this has not been done with regard to the position taken on social justice.

In one of his broadcasts, Mr. O'Reilly had this to say about social justice: "Leftwing zealots do not want any limits on spending- they want social justice. That means they want big money given to less affluent Americans through a variety of programs."[5] Never mind, as noted before, that big money has been given to large corporations through special tax breaks and through loopholes in the tax code. Are we to assume by Mr. O'Reilly's reckoning that it smacks of injustice when big money is given to the "less affluent" but just when it is done for the more affluent in the society? O'Reilly often fulminates against what he calls the "forced redistribution of wealth" and the massive federal spending on entitlement programs, but ignores the billions of dollars that have been re-distributed and loaded on to the wagons of the rich through hefty tax cuts and other incentive programs that directly benefit the rich.

In another tirade against social justice on his website, he adds further confusion to the subject by equating social justice with the progressive values of the political left. He accuses President Obama of pursuing a progressive, value-driven agenda and rants: "That means, the country's resources should be shared to elevate conditions for the have-nots."[6] Essential to this agenda would be high taxation to fund government run entitlement programs and welfare given with no strings attached. This welfare agenda according to O'Reilly, would ensure that the poor are provided with decent housing, good healthcare and money being spent on demand. The progressive agenda would also embrace "unfettered immigration and abortion" and working Americans should be "guaranteed a fair wage and generous benefits" by the government. He did not say whether these were laudable goals that any government would wish to pursue on behalf of its citizens, especially the weakest and more vulnerable. I give him the benefit of the doubt that he does believe that this should be the case, but attaching a social justice label to these in a politically derisive manner smacks of an ideology that completely misunderstands social justice, at least seen in its biblical perspective. It is counterproductive and should offend his Catholic Christian sensibilities.

Shorn of political ideology, fair wages worked in hospitable conditions, decent housing and proper healthcare are things that the Christian community,or an exceptional nation for that matter, should be concerned about. They are indeed subjects about which social justice speaks and occupy a prominent place in the struggle for social change. But in his confusion about the issue, O'Reilly is unable or unwilling to separate them from political ideology and so ends up diminishing their efficacy as serious social justice issues of which even he as a Christian ought to be concerned. Political ideology is allowed to trump serious Christian theology. As a service to his vast audience, Mr. O'Reilly would be well advised to study the lofty position that the social justice motif occupies in Roman Catholic thought especially in the writings of Thomas Aquinas and the papal encyclicals of John Paul, 11. There he will discover that the church teaches a preferential option for the poor based on clear biblical principles. This option is to be exercised in a practical and humane way in conformity to the will of God.

Before Glenn Beck lost his gig on *Fox News,* he used the program to trumpet misleading views about social justice. Unlike O'Reilly, he at least attempted to define more narrowly and precisely what he meant by the term. He trumpets that it is "forced redistribution of wealth with a hostility toward individual property rights under the guise of charity, and/or justice."[7] For him, the Troubled Assets Relief Program (TARP), the Obama stimulus, healthcare reform, financial bailouts, cap-and-trade, all have one common denominator: social justice. Under this definition, President Obama is branded a socialist and in some instances a Marxist, or as Mr. Beck once opined a man who hates white people (a statement he later recanted).

Beck encourages his acolytes to fiercely contend against this trend towards socialism and even encourages people to leave their churches if the pastor shows any orientation toward social justice. Pastors who believe in liberation theology are branded heretics as liberation theology is defined by conservatives as Marxism dressed up in religious garb. Never mind that liberation theology grew out of the struggle of Latin American pastors to lift the dignity of the poor and downtrodden often against tremendous acts of savagery from right wing dictators. Some of these dictators were clandestinely aided and abetted in power by the American government, especially in the period of the rule of the generals in the 1980's.

One does not wish to be too hard on these two gentlemen and neither should one second guess their Christian motives and commitment. But it is hard to reconcile their Christianity with their harsh polemic against programs that are intended to benefit the poor and why they seem so willing to deliberately mischaracterize social justice in such disparaging tones. Only recently O'Reilly referred to the food stamp program as one which encourages "parasites". Obviously the rich are not so characterized when they feed from the teat of generous tax cuts and subsidies which the poor will never have the privilege of getting. Is it that they do not know better or is it that they do, but they are just being disingenuous in order to fulfill a political agenda best known to themselves? If the latter is the case, then this would be most unfortunate because many people listen to them, especially to Mr. O'Reilly. By distorting social justice they are doing a great disservice not only to a lofty Christian tradition, but to their audience many of whom are church people. The sad thing is that many Christians do not seem willing to do any fact check on what is being fed to them by sources they consider authoritative.

Rush Limbaugh, and to a lesser extent O'Reilly, enjoy the longevity they do because a large constituency of evangelical Christians gives them succor. These Christians gullibly gulp down what they are fed and so become more and more paralyzed by the fear and anxiety generated by the redistributionist and class welfare rhetoric that comes from the microphones of these purveyors. As they continue to buy into this narrative the greater will be the division in the church and the less capable it will be in confronting the evils of the day which justice demands. As the social justice theme is distorted, much of the foundation that has sustained the viability of America over the years has been severely eroded and is in urgent need of repair or rebuilding. This calls for a united effort to tackle hard and intractable problems. But the country is deeply divided. A broken immigration system and abandonment of the social justice critique as an essential part of the nation's character, are just two elements of what is broken in America. In the next chapter we will examine further imperatives to be addressed as the country unites and gets engaged in the rebuilding process.

....

Notes on Chapter Three

1.Corrections Corporation of America (CCA) 2012 Annual Letter to Shareholders-under the signatures of John Ferguson, Chairman and Damon Hininger, president and CEO.

2. Tillich, Paul: *Love, Power and Justice*: (Oxford University Press, London, 1960), p.60.

3. Rahesh Kocher, Richard Fry and Paul Taylor: *Wealth Gaps Rise to record Highs Between Whites, Blacks and Hispanics*; Pew Research Center, July 26

4. Joseph Stiglitz: *Of the 1%, By the 1%, For the 1%*; Vanity Fair Magazine, May 2011.

5. Bill O'Reilly: *Moving to the Right?* Talking Points Memo delivered on the O'Reilly Factor, *Fox News*, on January 26, 2010.

6. Bill O'Reilly: *Progressive Values*, September 30, 2010, *Bill O'Reilly.com.*

7. *The Glenn Beck Show, Fox News Channel*, May 23, 2010.

CHAPTER FOUR

REBUILDING THE ERODED FOUNDATIONS

While the earnings of a minority are growing exponentially, so too is the gap separating the majority from the prosperity enjoyed by the happy few. This imbalance is the result of ideologies that defend the absolute autonomy of the marketplace and financial speculation.
(Pope Francis, Apostolic Exhortation, Evangelli Glaudium)

<<<<<<>>>>>

IF someone stood on the steps of the Lincoln Memorial on the morning of January 1, 2001 and predicted that by 2013 America would have elected a black president, the Supreme Court would have ruled same sex marriage acceptable, and marijuana would be made legal in some states, that person would have been declared either insane or seen to have abused a large quantity of hard drugs. Yet, this is where the nation stood at the end of 2013, a clear indication of how much the country has changed. These dramatic changes have been hard to accept by older members of the society who have become accustomed to a more traditional America. For some, the changes have been tumultuous as they have been frightening. But younger Americans believe their time has come and there is no turning back. They have entered into a new normal guaranteed by the new gadgets of technology and the facility of social media.

There are positive aspects to the changes that are taking place but there are also worrying trends of which a progressive society cannot be unmindful. For although we have made tremendous strides, the evils of racism, intolerance and bigotry continue to threaten the good order of society. In a culturally pluralistic society we have grown less accommodating of the diverse views that abound. Instead, there is growing belligerence, incivility and anger as each person seeks to protect his individual status quo. It is not just in our political discourse that we have seen this hardening of attitudes towards those with whom we disagree. Incivility has crept to the center of our social interactions and is standard fare for operatives in the media. We earlier alluded to the growth of hate speech and the frightening propagation of supremacist or hate groups in the nation as signals of the hardening of attitudes in the society.

It hardly needs to be said that this does not comport well with a nation that regards itself as exceptional. An exceptional nation would be cognizant of the cultural and demographic shifts that are occurring and prepare to meet them with openness and transparency. These demographic shifts are here to stay and they are destined to irrevocably change America as we know it. By some estimates, by 2050 America will be a brown society or at any rate minority racial groups will represent 50 percent or more of the population. As we approach these markers, the strength of America as an exceptional nation will be severely tested. There is enough to suggest that the test is already underway but so far the country does not seem to be doing too well at it.

This emerging reality disturbs those who would want to protect what is left of the old order. And America may well be witnessing the last gasps of that order. The defenders of a dying status quo do not give up easily and that is why we might be seeing the coarsening of social discourse in the public sphere as people push back or become territorial. Part of the reason for this opposition to change is fear-fear of what we might be losing and fear of what we may become. Fear is in fact the foundation of all our insecurities. As our insecurities increase, there will be a tendency to violence as people lash out in different directions to defend themselves. The process of social change has to be managed by accommodation and assimilation as people are helped to adapt to the changing social realities around them. This is something for the sociologists and social anthropologists to figure out, but reacting out of fear and violence is hardly the way forward. There is the urgent need to strengthen the common bonds that should bind all citizens together as they unite to rebuild the crumbling foundations. In rebuilding or strengthening these foundations, a number of imperatives need to be taken into consideration. I will assess a number of them here.

1. Closing the Inequality Gap

One of the most important factors that will spur a buildup of tension in the society is the growing inequality and the widening gap between the rich and the poor. There are those who will argue that economic inequality is an inevitable outgrowth of economic development; that it is a necessary consequence of the robust and intelligent deployment of capital and labor in a capitalist society. For them it is the difference between those who are prepared to take risk to invest their capital and talents for productive outcomes and those who are risk averse and who fail to use their talents wisely for their own personal advancement. Furthermore, as the argument runs, it is the vast difference between those who are prepared to work to dig themselves out of the ditch and those who are prepared to be takers-members of the Romney 47percent class. Ultimately, for them, it is the difference between those who value personal responsibility and those who are dependent on others and government for the fulfillment of their needs.

These may be cogent arguments, but they ignore the structural inequalities that have been built up in the system over the years and which prevent many from deploying their talents as they would wish. Often it is not that people are risk-averse or are dependent on government for help, but that there are structural inequalities which create obstacles that hobble and stymie entrepreneurial talent. One of the most glaring examples of this in recent times is the virtual shutting off of credit to small businesses in the aftermath of the 2008 financial crisis. It is not that people did not want to take risks but that the big banks that had benefitted handsomely from taxpayer generosity were not prepared to finance those risks. The monetary pipeline infrastructure that was established between Wall Street and the Federal Reserve in Washington never reached Main Street. Even today no real attempt has been made to build such an infrastructure and many small firms, which are the true employers of labor in the economy, struggle to survive. The lack of capital financing for these firms is one of the principal reasons for the sluggish growth in the economy.

It is therefore inappropriate and cruel to demonize people who cannot get a job as lazy as some commentators have done, when the decks are stacked against them. It is not that people do not want to work as some members of the Republican Party contend, but that the jobs are not available. And the jobs are not available because there has been no robust attempt by government since the first stimulus program in 2009, to come up with a credible job program or to otherwise stimulate the economy in the direction of job growth. The struggling unemployed get demonized for the failure and ineptitude of politicians in Washington.

It is clear that many in the struggling middle class do not have the connections or the lobbying power to milk the system as do the captains of industry and the well connected. Since the Great Recession it should have become evident that great income or vast wealth is not necessarily a result of smartness or entrepreneurial ingenuity. Often it is a function of how connected a person or corporation is to the seat of power; how agile these persons can be at buying political favors and loyalty by their lobbying efforts; and how ingenuous they can be in getting the system rigged to their own advantage. It is about being at the right place at the right time. Plutocratic wealth is also aided and abetted by tax loopholes which give the well connected advantages that the ordinary person will never have. The legislative agenda in many states often become hostage to powerful corporate interests. Some of these powerful groups may even write the agenda and hand it to politicians to rubber stamp. It is not farfetched to suggest that individuals who were not elected by the people may have more power over the elected to force their agenda upon an unsuspecting public.

The widening income gap between the richest and poorest members of society did not just happen by chance. It is a systemic problem that has been aided and abetted over the years by successive Democratic and Republican administrations that have pandered to special interest groups to perpetuate themselves in power. But a society that claims to be exceptional at home cannot be unmindful of this glaring inequality and the structures that support it. Neither can it sit at ease in an environment in which the top one percent has a greater collective net worth than the entire bottom 90 percent. In 2010 alone, 93 percent of the gain in national income went to the top one percent. The Gini Coefficient Index which measures household income inequality, noted that income inequality increased in the USA by 1.6 percent between 2010 and 2011. This is the first time that the index was showing an annual increase since 1993 and the highest since the Great Depression.

With the gradual decline in household income especially among the middle class, has come a corresponding rise in the poverty rate. In 2011 the poverty rate and the number of families in poverty were 11.8 percent and 9.5 million respectively.[1] This was not a significant change from the 2011 figures. It may be an index of the precipitous slide from the middle class into poverty that since 2010 half the population does not pay any income tax. They have fallen below the federal tax threshold either because they are unemployed or are employed but earning paltry incomes. There is a conjunction between the necessity for increased state welfare, joblessness and shrinking federal tax income.

The Farm Bill and the Food Stamp Program
The recent debate on the Farm Bill in the House reflects how difficult it is to arrive at any consensus in closing the inequality gap in the country. The bill has two major aspects, one dealing with subsidies to farmers and the other with nutritional support for distressed Americans through the Supplemental Nutritional Assistance Program (SNAP) [2]

commonly known as the food stamp program. The farm program itself has now morphed into another cash rich program for the rich and well connected farmers. In places like North Carolina, the Republican dominated state legislature has voted to end all food stamp programs. This action will make it decidedly harder for those who are unemployed to get the requisite nutritional help. Unemployment benefits have also been cut. When this is combined with loss of support from SNAP it is not hard to imagine the pain and suffering caused to those who genuinely need help and who are hardly making it.

The food stamp program is being cut across the country when people need it most. Statistics show that its usage has surged in recent times rising from 8.7 percent in 2007 to over 15 percent in 2013 according to the most recently available data. One of the criticisms of the Obama Administration is that the number of food stamp recipients has increased under his watch. While this is so, his detractors often fail to mention that with the advent of the Great Recession more people have fallen on hard times. Understandably, the federal government would be called upon to bear more of the burden to help these people.

Yet, Republicans heartlessly use the politics of mean-spiritedness to smear and dismiss these people as lazy, welfare recipients feeding from the troughs of a nanny state. But the rich who feed from the troughs of farm subsidy are not so characterized. There is a great deal of hypocrisy in a critique that focuses on gutting programs for the poor while upholding those for the rich. For example, Representative Stephen Fincher from Tennessee, who sits on the Committee on Agriculture, could not see any anomaly in his family receiving nearly 3.5 million dollars in farm subsidies from 1999 to 2012 and his virulent rhetoric against the food stamp program. To justify his rant by resorting to quotations from the Bible is not only poor exegesis but smacks of the kind of hypocrisy that Jesus would condemn.

Another part of the hypocrisy is that shown up in the criticism that one often hears that the food stamp program is riddled with fraud without hardly any mention that the farm subsidy program is also similarly bedeviled. In North Carolina, for example, federal officials described crop insurance fraud as "the largest crop insurance fraud scheme in the history of the program."[4]. In the recent Farm Bill debate in the House, Republicans, in their zeal to eliminate the food stamp program, frenziedly argued that fraud in the program was a centerpiece of their concern. Hardly a word was said about the corruption bedeviling farm subsidy. Yet, the Government Accountability Office (GAO-the investigative arm of Congress) has voiced serious concern that the level of crop insurance fraud might be understated.

At a House budget hearing in April 2013, Agriculture Secretary, Tom Vilsac, (whose department has responsibility for the farm subsidy and food stamp program), testified that even though the food stamp program is larger than the farm program, the percentage of error and fraud in the farm program were higher than in the food program. This is an inconvenient truth that should bring no comfort to the Republican ideologues in the House. It is disingenuous to use fraud as the basis of eliminating one aspect of a program because it is seen to be a drag on the country's budget, while upholding another aspect which may represent an even greater danger for the same reason. For those driven by ideology, it is social engineering when the poor receive help but signs of economic progress when the rich do. It cannot be state welfare when the poor get nutritional support from government and advancement for the national good when the rich do. There must be a balancing of the scales towards equity and fairplay.

It must be conceded that every big government program carries the risk for fraud and corruption. Corruption is often a feature of the expansive bureaucratic procedures which attend these programs. This is true of abuse in the Medicare program as it is of the humungous military bureaucracy. Any well-intentioned person must be concerned about such corruption and also about the danger of people becoming so dependent on state welfare that they no longer have an incentive to work. The Republicans are right in calling attention to this danger, but the way they have gone about correcting imbalances in the system is often to throw the baby out with the bath water in callous disregard for those who really need the help provided in these programs. The denial of unemployment insurance to those who need it in a sluggish economy is a case in point. So too is the denial of medical care to Medicaid recipients in many Republican states that reject the expanded Medicaid provisions of the Affordable Care Act.

A sad index of the growing inequality in the society is the increasing number of Americans who have come to depend on the federal government for income, food, student aid, housing and other forms of assistance. In the wake of cuts in the food stamp program and discontinuation of the extension of unemployment insurance benefits, the needs of the most vulnerable will increase exponentially. It is ludicrous to believe, as some members of the Republican Party do, that the void can be filled by charitable organizations. Since the economic meltdown, many of these organizations have come under tremendous pressure and are hardly coping. In any event, non-governmental organizations cannot substitute for what federal and state governments can and must do to help their citizens. It is an abdication of moral responsibility to think that they can as such thinking jeopardizes the care and health of needy Americans. Ultimately, America will be judged by how it treats its most vulnerable citizens in times of crisis and great need. In an age of growing inequality and festering discontent these needs are real; they are not mere abstractions.

Correcting the inequalities in our economic arrangements has got to be done carefully and with dispatch. Hope is fading fast especially for many in the middle class and those at the bottom rung of the economic ladder. Those who believed that under the Obama administration we would have been placed on the path to building a more equitable society have been disappointed by the lagging economy and the seeming inability or unwillingness of their elected leaders in Washington to do anything about it. Although the economy appears to be improving the quantitative gymnastics of the Federal Reserve many are not seeing any real improvement in their personal circumstances. When they go to the supermarkets, fill their gas tanks or do battle with the banks over ever increasing fees, they come to the realization that their lives are only being made more brutish and impoverished every passing day.

There are now signs that the president is seized with the urgency of placing the growing income disparity and inequality in the country on the national agenda. In his State of the Union address in January 2014, there was great expectation that he would have addressed the issue forcibly. But his speech with regard to this growing problem was tepid at best. The speech was bereft of any analysis of the structural impediments that have given rise to the growing income inequality, especially when this inequality has grown exponentially under his watch. There were no bold announcements of how these impediments are to be removed. MyRAs will not even cause a ripple in the stream of helping a struggling middle class to financial security. If people do not have jobs or if they are being paid low wages, their ability to save will be severely cauterized. A more fulsome presentation on the highly anticipated subject would have helped. The picture of the danger to the country of growing inequality could have been framed in 10 minutes of his speech. Lincoln gave the Gettysburg address in two.

Yet, despite the insufficiency of the President's speech in this regard, there are some on the right who have criticized him for stepping up the redistributionist rhetoric or for attacking the creators of wealth in an effort to stoke class warfare. But one is living in a fool's paradise if one feels comfortable with a situation where over the past 40 years 10 percent of Americans have corralled over 50 percent of the nation's income. If Republicans believe that this disparity is largely a function of single parenthood which can be corrected by marriage, or is an abdication of personal responsibility, or any variation of that theme, the illusion is even greater than one would have thought. Such notions, while they may have some bearing on the matter, simplistically ignore the structural impediments (such as a non-livable wage) which frustrate people's ability to be gainfully employed, work hard and stake their claim on their part of the American dream. To trumpet this rhetoric is in fact a disservice to their constituents, many of whom can hardly get by on what they are being paid for the hard work they do. If it were not such a serious matter it would be laughable that at a time when the President is being criticized for redistributing wealth to "parasites" in the economy, the wealthiest members of society have grown wealthier. To whom has the wealth been truly redistributed?

Yet, correcting structural income inequality cannot be done by simply redistributing wealth from the rich to the poor. A Robin Hood-type approach to inequality in which wealth is confiscated from the rich simply to give to the poor is not the way forward. This approach strengthens the resistance of the possessors of wealth as they seek to protect what they believe they have used their ingenuity and hard work to amass. It can exacerbate social tensions as the rich go into self-preservation mode. Furthermore, such policies may in the end do more harm to poor people than good.

While this must be acknowledged, it should also be patently clear that the problem of inequality cannot be solved by using governmental resources to enlarge the pockets of those who have special access to the wielders of political power and who have more than they can already spend. Pope Francis was right when he called attention to the depredations of the capitalist system which impoverish the many and expand the wealth of the few. Liberal commentators applauded his concern but conservatives fumed at what they saw as his assault on the capitalist system. But the Pope was not to be daunted. In a message addressed to participants at the annual World Economic Forum in Davos, Switzerland, in January 2014, the Pope challenged the business elite to put their wealth to the service of humanity and to not leave the world's population in poverty and insecurity. He observed that wealth should serve humanity and not be ruled by it. He declared:

> *The growth of equality demands something more than economic growth, even though it presupposes it. It demands first of all 'a transcendent vision of the person'. It also calls for decisions,*

mechanisms and processes directed to a better distribution of wealth, the creation of sources of employment and an integral promotion of the poor which goes beyond a simple welfare mentality.[5]

It is inconceivable that the Pope would ever be asked to be a participant at any "Davos-fest," though he would be a signal contributor to its deliberations. Meetings like these tend to lose their distinctive edge when they are predicated on economic determinism which is not buttressed by the moral imperative of concern for the person that should undergird them. This is where the Pope's call for a 'transcendent vision of the person' rings loudly. His call is in fact integral to the concern that the World Economic Forum has for the rising income disparity which it identified in its 2014 global risk assessment as the biggest threat to world stability.

In recognizing the foregoing, no one should suffer the illusion that a happy medium can be easily struck in trying to balance the needs of the poorer members of society with those of their wealthier counterparts. Those who are hoping for such a medium may be terribly disappointed. In America, the process is quintessentially a balancing act that has to involve robust legislation aimed at creating a more equitable playing field in which people are persuaded to play by the rules. Focus has to be placed on rural and urban poverty with emphasis on jobs, skill training and educational development. Urban revitalization has got be done systematically as in the approach being suggested for the revitalization of the energy sector.

Tavis Smiley and Cornel West are right in their insistence on a federal approach to the problem of poverty in America, but are naïve in thinking that because there is a black president there should be a greater effort to redirect resources to certain sections of the population. The approach to poverty has to be comprehensive and not selective. As the fight against poverty over the past 50 years has demonstrated, persistent poverty is very difficult to overcome. It is pervasive and its pernicious effects are felt throughout the society. This is why it has to be dealt with comprehensively, and not selectively, as a matter of governmental policy. The idea is to expand opportunity, to create the environment in which people's curiosity about an improved life can be inspired, especially the youth. This involves openness and freedom which leads to innovative thinking. Curiosity about a better life must become an indispensable component of youthful enthusiasm.

In the end, everyone, rich and poor alike, pay a price for persistent poverty. It is cold comfort to believe that you can live well in a society where a few are getting richer by the day while the poor are becoming poorer and are being pushed to the margins of society. A commonsensical view of survival should awaken anyone to the reality that persistent poverty is not only a morally offensive characteristic of any society, but builds a social powder keg which will one day explode. If this day should ever occur, to what extent can the rich consider themselves safe by barricading themselves in gated communities with the view that they will be safe from the disillusioned hordes who have had enough of squalor and degradation? Like the inequality which defines it, persistent poverty is a structural problem which can only be dealt with as the creative and innovative energy of the people, especially the young, is unleashed against it. For America, that spirit must be dominated by what Dr. King described as the fierce urgency of now.

2. Unleashing the Creative Energy of America's Youth.

Quite recently three young men aged 15, 16, and 17 shot and killed an Australian jogger in Oklahoma. When asked why they carried out this mindless act, one of them replied, rather nonchalantly, that they did it because they were bored. All around the globe youth is in crisis. From the youth protests in the United States and Europe to the rising tide of restlessness in the Middle East, there is a growing dissatisfaction among the young with how the world is being shaped and governed. Many have grown impatient with the status quo their parents have created. There seems to be an absence of adult mentorship to provide the social cohesion and continuity between one generation and the next. Instead what many young people see is a growing disenchantment among those who should be providing hope. Bereft of hope, many do not see any real possibility that their dreams and expectations can be productively met anytime soon. Disappointment and anger have boiled over into violence especially in the Middle East. The Arab Spring was itself a protest against dictatorial control as it was disappointment at unrealized dreams and expectations among the young.

> *A society will sooner than later feel the full fury when the creative energy of its young is consumed by indolence.*

The challenge to Western and Eastern societies alike is clear: how to harness the abundant energy of their burgeoning youth populations and channel this into productive outcomes which can circumvent the alternatives to violence that abound. An essential part of the answer lies in youth employment. No one has to be a social scientist to know that high youth unemployment leads to frustration and social tensions as creativity is stifled. There can be no greater danger to a society than to have a growing cadre of frustrated, unemployed youth in its ranks. Such a society will sooner than later feel the full fury when the creative energy of its young is consumed by indolence.

Even a cursory glance at the status of employment among the young in the United States does not present a pretty picture. The distressing statistics of rising unemployment among the nation's youth paint a dismal and worrying picture that is impatient of redress. In an analysis of statistics gleaned from the Bureau of labor Statistics, Sarah Ayres, a policy analyst at the Center for American Progress, reported that there are more than 10 million Americans under the age of 25 who are not able to find full time work.[6] Of this number over eight million cannot find full time work including over four million who are disconnected from both school and work and another 3.6 million who work part time.

In fact, part time work, especially among our young, is fast becoming a distressing feature of the American economic landscape.

Further analysis of the youth unemployment numbers reveals that close to 2.5 million of youths between the ages 16 to 19 are out of work or underemployed, while a whopping 8.2 million ages 20 and over are. Many in this latter group who are college graduates are either stuck in unpaid internships or have to settle for low wages and low skilled jobs. Many are boomerang kids who have returned home to ride out the storm.[7] There has been an increase in this category since the Great Recession.

A segment of the unemployed youth population that should be of particular concern to the society is those who are described as "disconnected" or "unattached" youth. These are neither enrolled in schools nor working. Those who are interested in working have to settle for menial jobs. There is hardly any prospect of educational advancement in this population, not to mention any possibility of vital work experience that can make them potentially viable citizens in society. This population of young people is the most likely to get involved in criminal activities, and some have. They too are most likely to depend on the government for state welfare.

Broadly speaking, youth unemployment cuts across all ethnicities, though Black and Latino teens are unemployed at an average of 32 percent, compared to whites at 21 percent. This is so even though Blacks and Latinos represent a smaller percentage of the overall teen population. The argument may be advanced that American youth unemployment is part of a global trend, as if it should not be taken as seriously as it ought. While this may be so, there is no compelling reason that America should be experiencing such a systemic decline in the productivity of its youth.

In the long run the nation will pay a price for prolonged youth unemployment. Already the negative effects of this phenomenon are being felt in the failure of many to repay their student loans with the attendant negative consequence of impaired credit and all that this portends for their future productivity. When vast numbers of young people remain unemployed there is a reduction in consumer demand, reduction in federal revenues, increase in crime and greater dependence on state and federal assistance. Without income they cannot save and so there is no prospect of a viable retirement. By far the most devastating consequence of youth unemployment is its debilitating effects on the spirit of the young at a time when that spirit should be most enthusiastic and vibrant.

While our political leaders play political games in Washington, too many of our young people remain idle. While they dither the vitality of the nation's future is being sapped. What is urgently needed is a broad-based, comprehensive program that effectively manages the transition from school to the workforce for disconnected youth. This would include an expansive and viable skills training program which can help them to adapt to new work environments. Germany's youth unemployment is among the lowest of any of the developed societies. This did not happen by chance. Before the Great Recession, Germany embarked on an ambitious and proactive skills training and apprenticeship program with private companies partly financed by the government. But in America this does not seem to be the priority. Political posturing and gridlock are the order of the day. As long as this state of affairs is allowed to exist, the more restless the nation's young people will become and the greater and more tragic will be the loss of its human potential.

3. Attending to the Moral Imperative of Good Governance

Peter Schweizer in his book, *Throw Them All Out*, asserts that America has been governed by the brightest political class in its history, yet the country has witnessed turmoil in the financial markets, an economy that was on the brink of collapse and the worst level of political dysfunction in its governance in recent memory. He posits that the problems the country faces are not related to a "smart gap" but to a "character gap;" not in ignorance, but arrogance. Jack Abramoff, who dealt with politicians in Washington more intimately than anyone else before he was disgraced, would agree with Schweizer. In an interview on *60 Minutes*, he narrated how easy it was for him to bribe politicians to get them to do his bidding.[8] It was nauseating listening to the interview because it brought out the stark reality of how lobbyists are able to easily influence elected leaders in ways that were against the public good. Furthermore, it brought out the extent to which the democratic process can be subverted by the highest bidder and how the vote of the ordinary person does not really matter in the exercise of political power.

It is not only in the United States that there is a moral breakdown in political leadership. The moral blight in political leadership is a virus which infects global political governance. A former president of a major European country can be indicted on a charge of sexual dalliances with under age strippers and yet harbor the thought that he could become president again. There is absent in Western societies the kind of moral and statesmanlike leadership that emerged after the Second World War.

Today's leaders are governed by a philosophy of what is expedient; they will not hesitate to fudge the truth or outright lie if it helps their cause. This is the character gap of which Schweizer speaks. Political action is rooted in what is convenient at a particular time, not in what is the morally right thing to do. It is rooted in relative thinking that believes that if one's action makes one feel good then do it. This is part of the reason why people have become disillusioned with the political process and why a country lurches from one crisis to the next. As one crisis is settled another erupts because firm decisions are not made that are consistent with firmly held moral principles of right and wrong.

With an absence of moral accountability comes poor governance. This applies to all three branches of government.

The Executive Branch
Despite his detractors, it would appear that the president is seized of the moral imperative that should undergird good governance. In his political career, there has been no personal sexual or financial crisis that the

president has had to confront or which have hobbled his presidency as has been the case with other presidents. Despite the hard work of Republicans and conservative groups to hurt his squeaky clean image, there have been no public scandals to link the president with any high moral failure. He has managed to maintain a profile of a stellar family man who has been able to stay above much of the corruption for which Washington has become well known.

> *The moral imperatives of good governance cannot be divorced from the pragmatism that should undergird it.*

But even the president would admit that the moral imperatives of good governance cannot be divorced from the pragmatism that should undergird it. It is this pragmatism that eluded the president in his first term and which was evidenced in his inability to forge consensus across the political aisle. His signature healthcare legislation was an epic achievement, but even this was accomplished without help from the Republicans whose greatest commitment is to see to its demise. It is true that without Republican obstructionism there is more that the president could have achieved especially in the areas of job creation and infrastructural development. But he too is without fault. In the aftermath of the Tea Party invasion of Congress in 2010, he and the Democrats seemed to have been surprised by the obduracy of this group and how effective they were in redirecting Republican politics along rigid, dogmatic lines. Towards the end of 2011 and well into the elections of 2012, they seemed to have resigned themselves to a narrative that nothing would get done by what had become a "do nothing" Congress. Even now, one of the prominent criticisms of the president is that his visible frustration at governance is his failure to work across the aisles of Congress, build consensus and forge compromise. To the extent that this criticism might be just, the president must be mindful that his efforts have to be more robust in this regard. He controls the bully pulpit and people expect him to get results. As president, he is best able to set the agenda, inspire people to rally around a set of well defined objectives, and lead in the accomplishment of those objectives. People are in no mood to accept excuses. He has to change the agenda.

There are some things that the president could do immediately to gain control over the national agenda and diminish the criticisms that he is laid back and is already behaving like a lame duck president. Since jobs preoccupy the national mood according to consistent poll data, he should reintroduce the comprehensive 2011 job bill. No recalcitrant politician can long resist the urgency of rehabilitating the crumbling infrastructure across the nation. The immoral position taken by those who would resist such an effort does not lie in the belief that this kind of work is necessary. They know that precious lives have been lost in bridges that have collapsed for lack of ongoing maintenance and that such efforts must be undertaken. Rather, their resistance is deeply rooted in a deep seated desire to see the president fail. And this is regrettable for to take this position is to play serious political games with people's lives and the nation's future. In any comprehensive jobs bill, emphasis must be placed on the middle class which is slowly dying, and in the employment of our youth as was earlier addressed. Comprehensive immigration reform must be an important corollary of a jobs bill.

Secondly, the president must not relent in his insistence that there will be no negotiation over any future raising of the debt ceiling. One hopes that he would have learnt the lessons over the past bruising battles and how much the nation's integrity was hurt by them. Since the last debacle with the Republicans over this issue, there are clear signs that he is winning the battle on this front. The nation has rejected the Republican scorched-earth approach to the issue. The economic imperative of the moment demands that debts that have been incurred and bills that need to be paid must be attended to. America must keep faith with its creditors and pay its bills. This is not just an economic imperative but a moral one. Those who would force the country into default must think very seriously about whose interest they are serving. One can be certain that it is not America's.

Thirdly, the crumbling education infrastructure must be addressed. America still boasts some of the best universities in the world but the country has fallen dangerously behind in its investment in critical areas of research, innovation and development. How can a national education enterprise be viable when it is made a hostage of sequestration especially in such a critical area as scientific research? How can optimal benefits be gained from a system which pays teachers low salaries, or lays them off, or which focuses on terrorizing students, teachers and parents into passing standardized tests instead of implementing methodologies that truly celebrate learning? Immediate answers to these questions may not be available but they are crying out for attention. On these and similar matters the president needs to draw a red line as to where he is not prepared to go. There is urgent need for a revamped educational system that punishes mediocrity and rewards curiosity, which is the best path to great learning.

Finally, he must lay out before the people a credible plan of what he wants to achieve for the next three years and enlist them on his side. One does not think that the president is naïve to assume that because his cause is just, righteous or moral people will automatically line up behind him to carry them out. By now he would know that he has to sell it to them and consistently follow up. In the matter of the Newtown shooting, for example, the president had over 90 percent of the people agreeing with him that there should be certain restrictions imposed on gun ownership including background checks. Yet, when the measure met defeat in the House as was expected, the president appeared crestfallen and seems to have given up the fight. The net result is that the momentum has been lost and people are still being killed in mass shootings. The president cannot afford to appear defeated for at any given time he has the hopes of an entire nation hanging in the balance.

The Congress

The Founding Fathers in their wisdom devised a system of government at the very heart of which was the principle of the separation of powers. This encompassed three branches of government-the Executive, Legislature (Congress) and the Judiciary-with distinct, legitimate and independent spheres of operation. This ensured that one branch could not exercise tyranny or hegemony over another. Since each sphere is independent, the system works best when decisions are arrived at by negotiation, consensus and compromise. If one part of the system should decide that it has no interest in compromise, then gridlock occurs with its unintended consequences for good or ill.

We have seen the ill effects of gridlock in recent times when the people's representatives take a studied decision not to compromise, but to oppose every bill or measure with which the Executive agrees. This is done even when those opposing the bill initially found favor with it but got jittery when the president did. There has to be trade-offs and one side cannot expect to get what it demands at the expense of the other. This simple fact seems to be lost on many of our policymakers. The answer to our economic dilemma cannot lie only with Republican insistence on tax cuts, cuts in spending or deregulation. Neither can it in Democrats insisting that short term spending or stimulus packages and wealth redistribution be the panacea for the ills of the economy. Oftentimes the answer lies somewhere in the middle where sensible deficit reduction is combined with selective spending in vital areas to spur growth.

Disrupting the smooth functioning of government in order to defund a settled law of the land, as in the recent debacle to defund the Affordable Care Act, is not only foolhardy but unworthy of legislators who have sworn to uphold the laws of the land. Furthermore, no political party should make the viability of a country's economy, and by extension the world's, a hostage to its own fortunes. Since the advent of the Tea Party to Congress, the Republican Party has gone down this road in the acrimonious debt ceiling debates that have thrown the country into unnecessary anxiety. All this is happening at a time when there is the urgent need for refurbished highways, safe water and sewer systems, coastal redevelopment and a host of other problems that have contributed to the anemic growth in the economy. There is urgent need for Congress to get beyond petulance and do the work that the country expects it to do.

One of the biggest reasons for American disaffection with Congress, and why that body continues to get poor ratings by the American people, is its petulant approach to compromise for the public good. Take the area of deregulation, for example, one of the pet areas for Republican obduracy. Despite the role that weak regulatory processes played in the recent financial crisis, there are still those who would like to see the removal of any regulation of businesses. The repeal of the Glass-Steagall Act under the Clinton Administration paved the way for mortgage derivatives (once described by Warren Buffet as "financial weapons of mass destruction"), to unleash their destructive fury on the economy thus precipitating the financial implosion of 2008. One would have thought that any responsible Congress would move with dispatch to enact legislation to prevent a recurrence of this problem.

It is true that the Dodd-Frank Act was passed with a view to correct the imbalances that had been built up in the system since the repeal of Glass-Steagall. But even now key provisions of the Act have not been implemented including the Volcker Rule which would restrict US banks from indulging in speculative investments. As is to be expected, the banks do not like this provision and are doing everything in their power, ably assisted by the Republicans, to delay it or to get total exemption from it.

Senators Elizabeth Warren, John McCain and Angus King who are pushing for a twenty-first century version of the Glass-Steagall Act are on the right track. The Act might not have prevented the devastation wrought by the financial collapse, but it certainly would have alerted regulators to the dangers that were being built up in the system. No legislation is without its imperfections but there is every suggestion that

Glass-Steagall would have significantly cauterized the impending implosion. Dodd-Frank also has its imperfections, but it cannot be argued with any rationality that the best approach is not to have any regulation, or to allow businesses to operate with impunity with self-policing functions, as the Tea Party zealots seem to be suggesting. The former Federal Reserve chairman, Alan Greenspan, would agree that good intentions did not prevail among big financial institutions in the lead up to the sub-prime meltdown.

If the recent financial crisis should teach any lesson it must be that no economy, whether under a socialist or capitalist orientation, can depend on the good intentions of people to do the right things. When it comes to making a profit the worst tendencies in the human heart tend to float to the top. There are those who will manipulate the rules or otherwise resort to abusive practices if this will ensure a robust bottom-line. They will seek to prosper at the expense of the poor, the unsuspecting, and the trusting by predatory behavior. Those who are inclined to behave in this way are not people to whom you can appeal by telling them to be patriotic. As Samuel Johnson so presciently warned, patriotism is often the last refuge of scoundrels. Yet, it is this sense of patriotism, respect and love for others that will make the difference between barbarism and anarchy and a cohesive society.

In critiquing the naysayers of regulation it must be stated emphatically that over-regulation cannot be the answer either. Just as in the struggle for equality, a careful balance has to be struck but that is where the problem often resides. It comes down to a question of who will be called upon to bear the greater burden: businesses that demand profit at any cost or the already harried taxpayer. If an idea for regulation is sound the rational approach cannot be to kill it on an altar of expediency, but to tweak and refine it to serve the greater good. In this is manifested the ultimate stupidity of the Republican Party zealots in their mission to destroy the Affordable Care Act.

In the end, legislations will be as effective as the agencies that are called upon by statute and emolument to enforce them. Powerful agencies such as the Internal Revenue Service (IRS) must not be allowed to become laws unto themselves. Every agency must operate with fairness and transparency and be alert to the evils that can be practiced under their watch whether by internal operators or people on the outside who only want to exploit the system for their own good. Many of the crises that have bedeviled key areas of government in recent times can be traced to laxity, complacency and slothfulness in agencies

> *However relevant a legislation, it will fail in the task for which it is intended if there are not agents with the required moral probity to implement it.*

that should have been wide awake in looking after the people's business. Crises are promoted and exacerbated by partisan appointments as people who are thus appointed are not necessarily able to exercise good judgments when called upon to do so. However relevant a legislation, it will fail in the task for which it is intended if there are not agents with the required moral probity to implement it.

In any event, the citizens have a right to demand that local, state and federal regulatory authorities be fair, balanced and transparent in their transaction of the people's business. They should not expect less and by their own vigilance should insist that these agencies be so governed. The failure of these authorities to function effectively for the public good is as much a function of the citizen's lack of vigilance about their operations.

The Judiciary-Supreme Court

As an important construct of how America is governed, the Judiciary plays a very important role in the interpretation of laws and in upholding the Constitution. No judicial system is perfect, but it can be said that the American judicial system has largely earned the respect and admiration of the American people. They cherish the independence of the judiciary as a counterbalance to the often arbitrary nature of the nation's politics. Despite its flaws people still depend on the judicial system for redress to their grievances and do expect the system to function in the best interests of the citizens it serves.

The Supreme Court stands at the apex of the nation's judicial system as the final arbiter in all manner of disputes. Over its long history debates have raged as to the proximity of the court to the political process. After all, the Supreme Court Justices are appointed by the President and ratified by the Senate. It is not farfetched to suggest that such appointments can be tainted by prevailing ideological orthodoxies. This has become a matter of great concern in recent times and is one about which a growing number of Americans have become uncomfortable. Ever since the Court's ruling in *Bush v. Gore* where one presidential candidate was favored over another, many have become disquieted about the court's impartiality. Other rulings since then have only widened people's discomfort that the court has become hyper-partisan especially in favor of the Republican Party. Conservative ideology is seen to be predominantly represented on the bench. People have a right to expect that decisions that are made on the high bench are consistent with the highest canons of impartiality recognizing how integral the Court is to the very survival of the nation.

The low ratings that the court now enjoys solidly reflect citizen disappointment that the court has been flirting too closely with partisan politics. For the first time in its history, the Court in 2012 fell below 50 percent in its favorability rating with the public. It is standing almost shoulder height with the Executive Branch but enjoys a more favorable disposition with the people than Congress. This falling esteem in which the Court is held cannot be good for the country. It cannot be healthy for good governance for people to lose faith in its chief arbitrator of justice. Often the court stands as the only bastion against injustice and oppression that can be exacted upon citizens by a tyrannical state. It often holds the collective security of people in its hands. Americans do not believe that the Supreme Court justices have to be flawless in their judgments or that they should not hold political opinions. As any citizen they have a right to their political opinions, but these opinions cannot be blatantly reflected in rulings as have become noticeable in recent times.

Needed: An Informed and Engaged Citizenry

The primary element of governance which gives real force and legitimacy to the ones aforementioned is an informed and engaged citizenry. Perhaps one of the most important lessons that should be learnt from the political gridlock in Washington is how the country's system of government is supposed to function; and how important a role the citizen has to play in its advancement or demise. It should have been brought home forcefully how really fragile is the democratic underpinnings on which it depends for its survival. It should have been a plain lesson in civics as to how government can be undermined and weakened by a politics of intransigence and obstruction.

If there is ever a time when the critical judgments and participation of an informed and engaged citizenry are needed, it is now. Prominent historian, David McCullough, is credited with the statement that an uninformed citizenry is fatal to democracy. This is a true statement which speaks to the need for people to make informed voting decisions. But it is not enough for people simply to be informed; they must become engaged as well. It is only as they are engaged that they can become factors for change.

As was stated earlier, one may not agree with the tactics of the Tea Party, but one of the things that gave their movement vitality was their willingness to move beyond outrage and stay engaged with the political process to bring change as they saw it. Their advocacy and agitation was a signal lesson in what is possible when a group of persons is willing to engage the political process with fixity of purpose. The Occupy Wall Street protesters were outraged about the widening gap between the one percent and the 99 percent, but failed to stay engaged to the extent that the movement now seems to have just petered out with only the 99 percent analogy left to remember it by.

Where the system is broken it would be sad that an informed and engaged citizenry cannot be called upon to fix it. It is true that with the political gridlock in Washington many have become disillusioned with the political process. But the answer to political dysfunction cannot be withdrawal or resignation but active engagement with the process to bring change. It cannot be enough for citizens simply to bellyache and curse the machinery of government as unworkable and then withdraw in protest and resignation. It befuddles the mind why anyone would want to vote for a candidate who poignantly declares and demonstrates that he or she is not interested in compromise when that is exactly what the system of government requires to get anything worthwhile done. The problem may not lie so much with the machinery of government or even with the representatives themselves, but with those who send them to the halls of power to represent them. Ultimately, people get the government they deserve and this could not be truer of the dysfunctional Congress we have today. In the end it is the informed voter that makes the real difference.

In the Citizens United ruling, the Supreme Court seemed to have operated on the assumption that an informed citizenry will make the right decisions or at any rate, decisions in its best interests when called upon to do so. It is true that the ruling has given corporations great advantage to influence election outcomes. Concern has to be expressed about their ability to do so, especially if you disagree with the belief that corporations are persons. In any event, corporations cannot vote, people do, but they have inordinate clout in flexing their spending power. The first real test of how they would behave in a national election was in 2012 when political Super PACs backed by wealthy individuals and supported by an avalanche of advertisements, were used to influence the vote. In the end it all came down to the sovereignty and sanctity of each person's vote. Sheldon Adelson, the Koch brothers or George Soros realized that they did not have any more votes at the booth than did the poor laborer from Arkansas.

The rejection of big money in the 2012 elections was a clear indication that people refused to be bought or to be unduly influenced by the rich. This in itself might be a perverse vindication of the Citizen's United ruling. The overkill of advertisements ended up annoying too many people. Too many of them insulted people's intelligence and by the time of the elections the people had had enough.

A particularly offensive advertisement was one carried by the Romney campaign which implied that Ohio jobs would be shipped overseas because the Obama administration had sold Chrysler to Italians who were now going to build jeeps in China. This was rated as the political lie of the year in some circles and yet it persisted for some time. People get more than a bit annoyed when they see big money trying to buy elections or when the rich flaunt their wealth in their faces. For all the money that poured into Karl Rove's Super Pac none of the candidates he supported were elected. There is no indication that the superfluity of advertisements influenced people to vote for Republican Party candidates in any significant way. What really motivated voters was the Republican strategy in some states to make it harder for people to vote or to otherwise obstruct the voting process. Coupled with this was the revulsion that many voters felt against the Republican strategy to obstruct and undermine the president in the performance of his work. They were not in a mood to reward this intransigence.

If people are informed and motivated to become engaged they can be counted on to vote in their best interests when the time comes. In this respect, one should not have to fear the gerrymandering of districts in Republican controlled states where districts are being re-drawn to give the Republican Party a distinct advantage at the polls. Again, it all comes down to the vote and what people perceive to be in their best interests. Those who contest for power must convince people as to what that best interest is. To achieve this they will have to educate the voter and get him sufficiently interested to go out and vote. That is, they must inform and engage the voter. This is how democracy works and this is how it has worked in America over the years despite attempts from time to time to re-define and disrupt it. There is no doubt that there is an urgent need for greater civic-mindedness among our citizens; for greater engagement with the political process. One may not like politics but it is one's civic responsibility to be informed and to get engaged.

The Responsibility of the Media to Inform and Educate
In a functioning democracy, media establishments play a critical role in the timely dissemination of information to the public. But, like the Congress, the Supreme Court, and Wall Street, the media rate poorly in the public's estimation. According to a Gallup survey of 16 institutions published in June 2013, public confidence in the media was at 23 percent, which was just three percent below banks and one percent above big business. Congress bore the weight for all of them at the bottom at 10 percent.[9] It should come as no surprise that a dysfunctional politics works hand in hand with a biased, dysfunctional media.

The media get poor ratings because they have become unreliable sources for good, hard and factual news. There was a time when media houses understood the critical responsibility of a free and unfettered press in the shaping of public opinion. This responsibility was buttressed by an ardent desire for objectivity and at getting to the truth about a story. The facts of a story were presented without embellishments. Commentary was based on empirical evidence instead of manufactured news to sell an opinion. Whenever a story was meant to be entertaining it was presented in a way that was neither crass, boorish nor divisive. Media houses have always had to focus on the bottom-line to keep afloat, but there was a certain integrity which imbued media practitioners and which allowed them to uphold the highest ethical standards of their profession often at tremendous pain to themselves.

But the media landscape has changed tremendously in recent times especially with the advent of the Internet with its blogging facilities and social media. In the competitive cutthroat environment in which it exists, the Darwinian principle of the survival of the fittest predominates. Journalists have been known to compromise their professionalism and to sacrifice truth and objectivity on the altars of personal ambition simply to survive. The angst is about ratings and growing income. As a result, hard news has become manufactured opinion. Reporters instead of reporting the hard facts about a story are more likely to offer an opinion

> *There is no greater morality that binds the professionalism of liberal media than does conservative.*

which is outside of their remit. Also, media houses have become very political in their dissemination of the news. There seems to be no inhibition to offer talking points given by influential corporations whose products they advertise or the political boss whose influence they wish to curry favor. And this happens on both sides of the media divide. There is no greater morality that binds the professionalism of liberal media than does conservative. In this competitive environment, vilification of other media practitioners has almost become normative. This contributes to the lack of civility in public discourse as guests are roughed up or called names in a sensational attempt to augment ratings. It is a game at which only the most astute and uncouth media practitioner seems to be successful.

In his commencement address at Harvard University in 1978, Alexander Solzhenitsyn critiqued the shortcomings of the Western press and of the American press in particular. He described hastiness and superficiality as the psychic diseases of the twentieth century and posited that these are manifested in the press more than anywhere else. He bemoaned that in-depth analysis was anathema to the press; that it was contrary to the nature of a press that merely thrives on sensational formulas. He was booed for his analysis partly because members of his audience did not think he had the moral authority coming from a totalitarian culture to lecture the Western press on its shortcomings. But how much has changed since Solzhenitsyn made those sage remarks?

In the competitive environment in which the press ekes out its existence, the public would be well advised to be very skeptical of what it sees, hears and accepts as hard, factual news. Although people ought to be more discriminating in what they accept as unvarnished news, the sad reality is that in a hard economic environment most people are too busy with their lives to spend time critiquing the news as they should. Their political bias will reflect the media house they trust for news. Few are willing or able to make a distinction between what is fair and balanced and what is spun to support a particular agenda. Change may only come when people become convinced that they have been betrayed by spin. The situation will only worsen as more people turn to the Internet for news. There, many will be lost and become entangled in a web of obfuscation, half truths and outright falsehoods.

In rebuilding the foundations of a great society, a free press that lives up to the highest canons of journalism is indispensable. The Founding Fathers recognized this when they enshrined freedom of the press in the Constitution as an indispensable component of a free society. The often undiscerning public must understand that they have a critical responsibility in keeping the press accountable. They must recognize the great power that the press wields in a free society and how much it can diminish their own freedom if they gullibly imbibe all that is fed to them. They must recognize that the press is ultimately accountable to those who use its services-the people. The people, not governments, are the ultimate censors of the press and the people should not make media owners forget this. Just as they should hold the politicians accountable so must they the press. With the turn of a dial, the press of a button, the tossing of a publication in the bin, the cancellation of a subscription or refusal to buy an advertised product, power ultimately resides in the hands of the people. But things will only change for the better when they refuse to allow themselves to be taken for granted and when they become more fulsomely engaged in what is going on around them. How they become and remain engaged will determine how exceptional a nation America becomes. To a discussion of the hallmarks of that exceptionalism we now turn.

....

Notes on Chapter Four

1. As defined by the Office of Management and Budget and updated for inflation using the Consumer Price Index (CPI), the weighted average poverty threshold for a family of four in 2012 was $23,364. See www.census.gov/poverty data).

2. SNAP may be a fitting acronym for the ways in which Republicans in Congress have attempted to snatch/ snap much needed support from the tables of poor families.

3. *Supplemental Nutritional Assistance Program Participation and Costs* survey-http://www.fns.usda.gov/pd/snapsummary.htm
4. Ron Nixon-*Fraud used to Frame Farm Bill Debate*-**New York Times**, June 17, 2013.

5. *Pope Francis Urges Davos Elite at World Economic Forum to Serve Humanity With Wealth*; **Reuters** report, Davos, Switzerland, January 21, 2014.

6. *America's 10 Million Unemployed Youth Spell Danger for Future Economic Growth*, **Center for American Progress**, June 5, 2013.

7. Boomerang kids are those who have graduated from college or university and have gone back home to live with their parents.
8. Lesley Stahl, *60 Minutes*, **CBS**, July 8, 2012.

9. *Confidence in Institutions*, **Gallup Organization,** June 1-14, 2013.

CHAPTER FIVE

THE SHINING CITY ON A HILL

I've spoken of the shining city all my political life....And how stands the city on this winter night? After 200 years, two centuries, she still stands strong and true on the granite ridge, and her glow has held steady no matter what storm. And she's still a beacon, still a magnet for all who must have freedom, for all the pilgrims from all the lost places who are hurtling through the darkness toward home. (**President Ronald Reagan in his farewell address to the nation on January 11, 1989**).

There is something evil in our society that we as Americans have to work to try and eradicate (**Dr. Janis Orlowski, in a statement made after the Navy Yard shooting in Washington**).

I have been given to understand how small this world is and how it torments itself with countless things it need not torment itself with, if people could find within themselves a little more courage, a little more hope, a little more responsibility, a little more mutual understanding and love (**Vaclav Havel, Harvard Commencement Address, May 12, 1995**).

<<<<<<>>>>>>

The phrase, "city upon a hill" was coined by John Winthrop, a Puritan pilgrim, in a sermon delivered in 1630. As pioneers, Winthrop and his fellow pilgrims had no idea what they would make of the new land to which they had come. But there was one thing that pulsated in their hearts and it was the optimism that they could create a society that would be a model to the rest of the world; a beacon that would draw people to its shores. It would be a city upon a hill which, in the words of President Reagan almost three hundred years later, would be a magnet for all who desired freedom.

The first pioneers to America felt that they had come to a place which was different. Instinctively they felt it would provide opportunity which was grounded in the optimism that they could carve out a society much better than the one they had left behind. Distance and geography would shield them from the tyranny from which they fled. Deep down they felt that the freedom that had been denied them at home could be found in this new land. They could now pursue their manifest destiny as the Creator gave them succor. The fecundity of their imagination allowed them to see a bright future ahead. It was a future fraught with danger but which could be built by faith in the God they believed had led them to this place. It is out of a crucible of hope for a free society that the American experiment began and what a journey it has been. Today the experiment continues and each generation of Americans is challenged to keep the lights on in the city or face the danger of it being tragically extinguished altogether.

An Exceptional Nation

To set our discussion in perspective it may be necessary to begin with what could be considered the marks of American exceptionalism. With the perceived decline of America, some people would not consider this term descriptive of where America is today. Yet, there are those who speak proudly of the country in these terms and who believe that there is just something about America that makes it stand out among the nations of the world. There is a feeling among those who believe in America's greatness and among many who yearn to come to its shores, that there is something special about the country, Vladimir Putin's broadsides against such a notion notwithstanding. Throughout this book emphasis has been placed on the necessity of keeping America exceptional. Here we will look more closely at what are the defining marks of this exceptionalism.

In his book, *Democracy in America* in 1831, Alexis de Tocqueville extolled the advanced nature of American democracy compared to that of its European counterparts. In his travels around the country, he was deeply impressed by how democracy pervaded every nook and cranny of American life; how alive the democratic sentiment was and how it made for a well-ordered society. He was particularly impressed by immigration and how people from all over the world with their diverse cultures, could come to America and be assimilated into a dynamic experiment of nationhood.

There can be no doubt that this ability to absorb people from every clime and culture around the world is still one of the bedrock principles of what defines America as exceptional. The importance of immigration to the American project was already assessed, but it is important to reiterate that the xenophobic rhetoric of recent times does not spell well for making America a special place for people to come. The uniqueness of America as a truly immigrant nation unlike any other is an integral part of any understanding of the nation as exceptional. Any attempt at reforming immigration must understand this and must be in tune with the global consensus that in America you can make a better life for yourself and your family.

In considering the marks of American exceptionalism, a number of things may be noted:

1. America is not Exceptional Because of its Military Might.

The concept of America as an exceptional nation is not grounded in a philosophy of might being right or in any vaunted belief that the country can muscle its way through the world. Wary and cautious presidents have well understood the limitations of American military power in global affairs. Perhaps the most prominent in recent times was Dwight D. Eisenhower, himself a man of superb military status, and easily one of the most decorated military persons in America over the past 50 years. In his farewell speech to the nation in 1961, Eisenhower sounded the warning about the danger that could be posed by what he described as the rising military industrial complex. He could see the dangers for he was in the center of it both operationally as a general and field commander, and administratively as President. In the speech he acknowledged that despite the "holocausts" to be seen in the wars in which America had been engaged, America in 1961 was still the strongest, most important and productive nation in the world. He acknowledged that America should be proud of this pre-eminence, but went on to make the sober statement that:

> *America's leadership and prestige depend not only upon our unmatched material progress, riches and military strength, but on how we use our power in the interest of world peace and human betterment…Crises there will continue to be. In meeting them, whether foreign or domestic, great or small, there is a recurring temptation to feel that some spectacular and costly action could become the miraculous solution to all current difficulties.[1]*

The "spectacular and costly action" of which Eisenhower spoke, has resonance for the country's costly adventurism in Iraq. This costly action, both in blood and treasure, was indulged in because, again in the words of Eisenhower, we did not weigh our response "in the light of a broader consideration." And what was this broader consideration of which both the President of the United States, George W. Bush, and the Congress which authorized the war, should have been mindful? It certainly should have been the need "to maintain the balance between cost and hoped for advantage; between the clearly necessary and the comfortably desirable."[2]

It was a failure to maintain this balance on the part of the Bush Administration that plunged the nation into an unnecessary and costly war founded on the false assumption of a few influential persons, including the Vice-President, that American exceptionalism would be vindicated by its military might. American troops would be greeted with garlands in the streets of Iraq. There was not even the need to have an overwhelming military force as the Powell doctrine counseled. The rag-tag Iraqi army would be a pushover.

The logical outcome of this hubris was the belief that pre-emptive strikes against an enemy, however weak, could be done even if there was no great moral clarity that America's fundamental interests were threatened. This is a position that American global diplomacy had hitherto frowned upon for good reason. Buttressed by a notion of unilateralism, it carried the dangerous overtones of the imperial presidency. The notion that America could go it alone, that it could do anything in the world regardless of what others may think, was itself un-American.

What was absolutely alarming in the president's rush to war was the absence of what one would describe as the "presidential pause." Whenever a president is faced with a decision that will have far reaching consequences for the nation, especially in committing the nation to war, there is personal deliberation on his part, a kind of pause in which he gives himself time to reflect so that he can be reasonably assured that the course he is about to embark on is the right one to take. This is almost a sacred moment for him, an anguish of the soul, as he ponders the weight of the issue and its possible consequences for the nation. There is cold comfort to the thought that Bush Junior committed himself to this moment. When faced with the decision to embark on Desert Storm, even though the situation at the time had strong compelling moral force, his dad, Bush Senior, had this pause.

Bush Junior must have known that the intelligence to go to war in Iraq was not compelling in terms of that nation possessing weapons of mass destruction as had been adjudged. Indeed, the intelligence was suspect as Mr. Rumsfeld has now admitted in his book, *Known and Unknown*. After the Congress had given him permission to proceed if he considered it necessary, the ultimate decision became his. But he was not deterred in his decision to proceed. History has already started to make its own judgment on this decision.

It is amazing that Britain allowed itself to be pulled into this reckless adventure in Iraq. Former Prime Minister Tony Blair, sarcastically dubbed "Bush's poodle," tried desperately to defend British action before the parliamentary Commission of Enquiry into Britain's involvement in the war. It did not go too well for him. Whatever spin might be placed on Britain's involvement and that of the USA, the incontrovertible fact remains that in dethroning a dictator and a perceived enemy of the West, a cradle of human civilization has been permanently scarred, and we are no more safe as a people for it.

In fact, America's reputation around the world was sullied as a result of this adventurism. The world saw a side of America that it did not like; it was not a proud moment for American exceptionalism. Even today, in the aftermath of our involvement in Iraq, skeptics and critics alike assail any notion of American exceptionalism on the basis of what Iraq has become because of America's involvement there.

Furthermore, not having made the distinction between the clearly necessary and the comfortably desirable, the war was undertaken at a very high cost to the American people. Up to the point when active combat ended, over 4,200 American servicemen and women had been killed; over 30,000 have been injured and different surveys put the number of Iraqi civilians killed at between 110,000 and 150,000 between March 2003 and June 2009. These statistics cannot account for the continuing pain and burden to family members of those killed and injured and whose lives have been maimed or otherwise disrupted. Neither can they account for the psychological deficits registered in the lives of those suffering from post traumatic stress disorders (PTSD) and other mental illnesses directly attributable to the war.

Apart from these personal costs the monetary cost of the war has been staggering. In an Op-ed in the *Washington Post* on September 5, 2010, Nobel Laureate and renowned economist, Joseph Stiglitz along with Linda Bilmes, the Daniel P. Moynihan lecturer in Public Policy at Harvard University, put the total cost of the Iraq war to the US at three trillion dollars.[3] This does not include the cost for the war in

Afghanistan. This estimate completely dwarfs the Bush Administration's estimate of over 50 billion dollars at the start of the war in 2003. The writers rightly contend that the war has added to the federal debt and suggest that it was a factor in the financial collapse in 2008. The war was engaged at a time when the Bush Administration, rubber stamped by a willing Congress controlled by Republicans, gave the biggest tax cut to date to the richest one-tenth of the population. Never before in the history of American wars was a tax cut given when war was being waged in two separate territories.

It meant that the war was conducted on borrowed money and the country is still feeling the pain of this misguided adventure. The pain is felt in the soaring national debt which has moved from 6.4 trillion dollars in 2003 to over 10 trillion dollars in 2008 when the global recession began, to over 17 trillion dollars today. The ballooning debt and deficits built up by the unpaid for wars were undoubtedly important factors which precipitated the financial collapse in 2008. The continuing health costs and disability payments to veterans is estimated to add another trillion dollars to the debt.

Despite the stout defense of the war that Bush has mounted in his memoir, *Decision Points*, the facts remain that this expensive foray in Iraq will continue to haunt the treasury for years to come. Did the president regret going to war in Iraq? In an ABC television interview just before he left the White House, the president remarked that the greatest regret of his presidency was to have gone to war in Iraq on flawed intelligence. There was no clear answer to the question as to whether he would have done so had he known the intelligence was flawed. Yet, in the words of Cabinet member Paul O'Neill, there was an obsession with Iraq very early in the Bush presidency.

The entire world witnessed the tortured presentation given by the unwilling Secretary of State Colin Powell at the UN to convince the world why Saddam should be taken out. The secretary's role in the events leading up to the war is still befuddling. The Secretary clearly was not convinced that the information he was presenting to the UN was one that was supported by the best intelligence from the CIA. That is why he requested George Tenet, the CIA director, to sit directly behind him during the presentation. When he told Bush that attacking Iraq would leave a broken country that he would end up owning, it was the moment when he had the greatest opportunity to demonstrate the statesmanship of the office he occupied and resigned.

He should not have allowed himself to be bamboozled by a Commander-in-Chief and his underlings to make a presentation about which he obviously had fundamental, philosophical doubts, if not disagreement. Resignation would have forced the Administration on its hind legs, and maybe, just maybe, the president might not have gone to war. It would have given him the "presidential pause" that he needed to make. Public debate would perhaps have become more trenchant and the Secretary would have won public admiration for his decision. But the Secretary failed to make the distinction between his function as the Secretary of State and that of being a well decorated general who was loyal to his Commander-in-Chief. Faced with the choice of staying or resigning he defaulted to the military option and stayed on in deference and loyalty to his Commander-in-Chief and at variance with his own conscience. Today, whenever he has to address the issue of Iraq, he appears pained and broken. His redemption may yet come in a brief memoir in which he tells the truth, and nothing but the truth, about the whole matter.

There can be no doubt that in recent American history, the Bush presidency represents the greatest challenge to American exceptionalism as it has been traditionally defined and as we have sought to define it in this book. The administration and those who subscribe to a notion of exceptionalism based on military might confuse Tocquevillian exceptionalism with imperialism. The idea of the imperial presidency held sway in Iraq and this was anathema to the American character. America might not have been interested in nation-building in Iraq as the administration truthfully claimed, but this became one of the unintended consequences of the war. Nation-building in the context of military conflict, especially in urban settings, is not in the American DNA; it is not true to the American character.

When necessity was forced upon the country to own what it had broken (as Powell had presciently warned the president), the nation had to undertake the rebuilding of Iraq. From the early stages of the rebuilding process this job was done poorly. Billions of dollars were spent without the necessary mechanisms of accountability to govern such spending. Handpicked, no-bid contracting became fashionable and yet there were no proper systems of accountability and transparency to give the necessary oversight that could restrain and punish the greedy and minimize mediocrity and corruption. The lives of ordinary Iraqis were further disrupted by rank incompetence in doing even the most rudimentary infrastructural project. Incompetence and corruption were the defining features of many a project.

The country seems not to have learnt its lessons from the Iraqi experience as corruption and incompetence continue apace in Afghanistan. It may not be possible to quantify the amount of waste of taxpayers' money that has gone on in the rebuilding efforts in both countries. The truth, which would not be easily admitted by those who stoked the fire of war, is that America does not have any skill sets in rebuilding a war torn nation or for that matter in Urban guerilla warfare. The damage to Iraq by the sustained failure of the rebuilding process was further exacerbated by the absence of these competencies.

Whatever success the defenders of the war in Iraq may boast about, the undeniable reality is that too many lives have been lost there, property destroyed and people's livelihood dislocated in a war in which clearly the country should not have been engaged. There is a clear role for the American military in supporting a notion of American exceptionalism, but it must be one confined to humanitarian efforts as in the prevention of genocide in the Balkans under Clinton. A case could also be made for the pre-emption of wholesale destruction of lives under a brutal dictator, as in Libya under the emerging Obama doctrine of US unilateral intervention in preventing genocide or any mass slaughter of a civilian population. Such intervention must be in defense of American core values of preserving freedom and an unswerving commitment to the rights of all people to self-determination. It must be hoped that never again will America define its exceptional character in military language but in a language that seeks peace. That is the kind of America that one can believe in.

2. American Exceptionalism is Deeply Grounded in its Partnership with the World.

When President Obama came to office American respectability around the world was severely diminished. This was fueled largely by America's involvement in Iraq which fed the perception of America as an arrogant bully motivated by a unilateralist approach to world diplomacy. Since the G.W. Bush Administration, many have looked more critically at America's role in the world. In almost every country across Europe, Asia, the Middle East and Latin America, Americans have been viewed with suspicion and in some Arab countries with downright hate.

One of the first tasks of the Obama presidency was to seek the restoration of America's standing in the world. The president started with some targeted speeches aimed at the Muslim community. The most important was given at Cairo University in June 2009 when he called for an end to the Arab-Israeli conflict and outlined America's hopes for a strong and vibrant relationship with the Muslim world. Many of his detractors on the conservative right, who believe that America's exceptionalism can only be sustained by hard power, criticized him for conceding too much to the Muslims and for weakening America's standing in the world. They accused him of apologizing to the world, an attitude they consider unworthy of any American president. The hostility toward the president generated by these accusations only served to fuel the paranoid assumptions of the far right that he is a Muslim who was not born in America.

What the Obama Administration recognized from very early is that America's strength in the world is best seen in its use of "soft" power as former Harvard professor, Joseph Nye, so eloquently defined it in his book: *Soft Power: The Means to Success in World Politics*. The deployment of American soft power speaks to its ability to attract others by its values and by the policies that are based on those values. America is weakened in the eyes of the world when these values are retrenched by the country using force to impose its will on people. Those who contend that people hate America because they envy the way Americans live and their prosperity often miss the more important point that the world resents America when it is perceived to be acting like a bully.

Speaking to journalists in Strasbourg, France, the president rightly acknowledged other nations' right to regard themselves as exceptional. Even this basic acknowledgement did not go down too well with some of his more persistent critics. The President went on:

> *I see no contradiction between believing that America has a continued extraordinary role in leading the world towards peace and prosperity and recognizing that that leadership is incumbent, depends on our ability to create partnerships because we create partnerships because we can't solve these problems alone.*[4]

This concession of the need for partnership with the rest of the world is a theme with which the president has been very consistent. He reiterated this theme in his most recent speech to the United Nations General Assembly:

> *Objectives can rarely be achieved through unilateral American action, particularly through military action. These objectives are best achieved when we partner with the international community and with the countries and peoples of the (affected) region.*[5]

He recognized that the international community has depended on America to use the sacrifice of its blood and treasure to stand up for the interests of all. But he acknowledges that this is not a burden that America can bear alone:

When American interests are not directly threatened, we stand ready to do our part to prevent mass atrocities and protect basic human rights. But we cannot and should not bear that burden alone.[6]

Mindful of criticism of America as the world's global policeman, the president was very careful in his remarks to give clarity to the limitations of American power in the world. In what could be an emerging Obama doctrine on America's intervention in global affairs, the president was clear about the dangers of America disengaging from the world:

The danger for the world is not an America that is too eager to immerse itself in the affairs of other countries but that it may disengage, creating a vacuum of leadership that no other nation is ready to fill.[7]

Or, quite frankly, is capable or willing to fill. These sentiments which form a core philosophical construct of the Obama presidency, no doubt profoundly disturbs those who believe in American unilateralism. Those who protest the president's new posture seem unwilling to accept that things have changed; that technology has shrunken the entire world into a global village. The clout that America once had in the kind of expansionist world envisaged by unilateralists is no longer sustainable or can be taken for granted. As the war against global terrorism has shown, American security in that shrunken global environment cannot be necessitated by America going it alone or using military muscle to ensure the security of its citizens. Smarter and more respectable ways have to be found to ensure that security. The best insurance Americans can have in this changed environment is a resurgence of the nation's core values that have sustained her over the years.

The bottom-line is that the world needs America and America needs the world. This calls for the building of coalitions of support and partnerships that the president spoke so eloquently about in Strasbourg and in his speech to the Muslim community in Cairo. In any case, the country no longer has the kind of resources that the exercise of hard power demands. It cannot continue pushing hard power on rising deficits and a runaway national debt, or to put it bluntly, on the backs of the fiscally prudent Chinese. There is a point where common-sense if not internal logic demand that it re-examines its use of hard power. In this re-examination it would help to recall Eisenhower's farewell speech in which he warned against the rising military industrial complex. It was precisely in the context of America's role in world peace that he made an impassionate declaration of concern for what he saw as the "unwarranted influence" of the military industrial complex:

> *This construction of an immense military establishment and a large arms industry is new in the American experience. We must guard against the acquisition of unwarranted influence, whether sought or unsought, by the military industrial complex. The potential for a disastrous rise of misplaced power exists and will persist.[8]*

It is the persistence of this misplaced power that soft power has to resist if not neutralize. We have seen the persistence of the military industrial complex to alarming levels of cost that not even Eisenhower with his admirable imagination could have envisaged in his sobering speech. Today, more money is spent disproportionately on defense than on any other item in our national budget. No politician can make it to Congress who does not sound strong on defense. Former Secretary of Defense, Robert Gates raised alarm at the high cost of maintaining the defense department. His suggestion to cut the defense budget in some key areas was met with strong opposition especially in districts that depend on defense contracts to provide employment. But one does not have to look too far to see that America's defense industry has become one massive, cumbersome, lumbering giant hobbled by bureaucratic inertia in many areas. Robert Gates was right: America has to move from a culture of endless money to a culture of restraint. But who is brave enough to bell this cat?

3. American Exceptionalism is Based on a Culture of Compassion and Social Justice.

We have already surveyed the imperative of compassion and social justice as being essential to what America is or ought to be. Here we will examine more precisely how this notion applies to her as an exceptional nation. Despite the biting criticisms that America often receives from the world, there is almost the instinctive belief that the country can be counted on to give formidable assistance in a time of global crisis. This is something of which Americans ought to be proud. There is no other country on the planet that can mobilize global compassion than America can. When there was carnage and genocide in the Balkans, America was counted on to respond along with NATO forces to end the atrocity there. The Clinton Administration was severely criticized for inaction in the wake of the Rwandan genocide. At the heart of this criticism was the belief that America could have prevented it and should have intervened to prevent it.

Despite its pretensions to the contrary, the world has grown accustomed to American generosity in times of crisis. America responds not because the world necessarily expects it to, or because it has the resources and logistical infrastructure to do so. It does so because such generosity has been woven into the nation's DNA from its founding. The truth is that per capita America is the most generous nation on the face of the earth. This is the kind of America that the world knows and that is why the foray into Iraq left many people around the world befuddled. Such reckless, military adventurism was a violation of the better part of the American soul.

Whatever America's perceived role in the world, the greatest characteristic of American exceptionalism is first and foremost grounded in how well Americans treat each other at home. American exceptionalism is never a foreign construct. It is particularly seen in the area of social justice and how we care for those who for no fault of their own can no longer do so. This compassion extends to the rest of the world as it embraces the fairness with which the country treats those who for various reasons brave hardships and come to its shores seeking a decent life. They come because they believe that in America they can make one last stand for their life's dream which eluded them in the country of their origin.

Charity, it has been well said, begins at home. If this is a correct assessment of what American exceptionalism ought to be, then there are worrying signs that we are fast losing this distinctive edge. At a time of growing disillusionment, many have become convinced that America is no longer the caring and nurturing society it should be. There are good reasons for this growing pessimism in light of the glaring income inequality in the society, the rising poverty rate as many in the middle-class descend into poverty, and the dysfunctional politics that has imposed a great deal of unnecessary hardship and stress on the society. Many feel isolated from the mainstream as they see more of the nation's resources going to the few and the many just being able to scrape by month after month. For many, each month begins as it ends: mammoth bills to be paid without a sign of any jobs to give them a more hopeful future.

There are many to whom the words "life, liberty and the pursuit of happiness" in the preamble to the Declaration of Independence ring very hollow. For them life is a constant struggle in which they are not able to reconcile the discrepancy between a country that has such abundant resources and one in which so many are poor. The gap between the haves and the have-nots, as noted before, has widened considerably. In some big cities there are depressed neighborhoods that depict life in Third world societies ruled by tin pot dictators. Despite the assumptions of the newly enacted healthcare reform act that healthcare is now widely affordable to citizens, many have to decide whether they go to a doctor or remain home and die. If they do go, they have to calculate whether to buy the medication or half of it or to buy food. This is a

137

glaring indictment on a society that prides itself in being exceptional. No one expects to see these conditions in America yet, sadly, it is a way of life for too many of her people.

Social justice and compassion are not just social constructs but essential ingredients in what goes into making America exceptional. In recent times there have been serious challenges to these principles and they have been accentuated by the great recession that hit in 2008. There is a crass materialism and rugged individualism built upon greed that has entered the public square in a way that many have not seen before. Greed is not a vice that is new to the American character. Greed resulted in the decimation of the culture of the native Indian population in the search for gold and the harnessing of land by white settlers. Greed led to the perpetuation of the institution of slavery which persisted under the US Constitution for almost 78 years when it was finally abolished by the 13th amendment of the US constitution on December 6, 1865.

Of more recent vintage, greed led to the collapse of the financial sector and triggered a global recession from which the world is just slowly recovering. Greed, according to Gordon Gekko in *Wall Street*, is good. Good perhaps for the "janitors of the status quo" who are able to position themselves to benefit from it. It is certainly not so for those whose lives have been negatively affected by having to live the indignity of unemployment, of not being able to feed their families or who have been made homeless by foreclosures.

The sad truth is that with the recession has come a callous disregard for persons. A glaring characteristic of this disregard is the absence of a desire to do justly by others. The poor feel ripped off by unconscionable banks and no one seems to care. Despite the Affordable Care Act, the delivery of healthcare is very costly and does not appear to be based on a person's ability to pay but how much profit can be made on the backs of the suffering. Hospital fees in many jurisdictions are unconscionably high and often bear no resemblance to treatment given. Sentences are handed down in courts that clearly demonstrate the divisibility of justice; that there is a justice for those who can pay the highest price and one for those who cannot. And those who cannot pay are often locked away in a prison industrial complex with little regard for their unalienable rights. We seem not to realize that the high cost of justice is justice denied; that where there is an absence of social justice there is anger.

The most recent shutdown of the government and the rancorous debate over the raising of the debt ceiling, have left many Americans with a bitter taste in the mouth and a more distrustful view of their governors. The low ratings given to politicians in Washington continue apace and are consistent with governance that does not seem to care, at least as far as a growing majority of Americans are concerned. There was a time when policymakers from both parties would unblinkingly respond to ease the sufferings of Americans who fall on hard times, but nowadays there are prevarications and obstructions placed in the way of getting bills passed that could help the more vulnerable citizens. Contrary to the views of some in the media who should know better, most Americans do not think that they are entitled to be given things. The last thing that many would want is to live off government handouts. Most work hard so they can get a fair shot at the American Dream. It is an insult to their intelligence to tell them that they are exploiting the system because they happen to fall on hard times. American compassion, before the arrival of the Tea Party in Congress, has always mandated generosity to these people. They should

> *The extent to which a nation cares for the most vulnerable in its midst is the best test of its character as an exceptional nation.*

rightly expect some cushion from government so that they do not hit the pavement too hard. This is not to advance a progressive agenda as some on the right, both in media and the Republican Party, have asserted. It is the citizen's expectation of what a decent government should do on their behalf in a time of need. This is social justice, not a decadent socialism or rabid Nazism. This is what an exceptional nation does for its own. The extent to which a nation cares for the most vulnerable in its midst is the best test of its character as an exceptional nation.

A Tolerant Society?
Americans often pride themselves in being a tolerant society, but honesty should admit that citizens have grown cruder in their behavior to those who look different from them or who do not share a particular view of how the society should be governed. Talks of secession abound in some states and the growth of hate groups is fast becoming an industry and a big headache for the federal investigative authorities. The perceived need by many Americans to arm themselves is fodder to this hate industry as it surrenders to the growing fear that Americans have that they have to protect themselves from enemies real or imagined. The neighbor from whom one could get a pinch of salt is now regarded with suspicion especially if one does not hold his or her political or religious views. We speak glibly of being a tolerant society but the evidence is that instead of being a kinder and gentler society we have grown less compassionate and more crass and bigoted in our regard for others.

What is unfortunate about all this is that these attitudes are becoming entrenched in society at a time when the demographic reconfiguration of the society has picked up pace. Sanity would dictate that we grow more tolerant and respectful of the differences in persons. It is true that political dysfunction has hardened the intolerance that we are seeing, but what is emerging goes beyond politics. It may very well reflect what we are fast becoming as a society. Is it possible to imagine a time when the specialness of America for which many would give their lives may be replaced by a notion of the ugly society from which they would rather flee? The question might not be as farfetched as it may sound or appear. But if fleeing should be the futuristic answer it would be a cruel irony, for it would indicate that America is no longer that welcoming place that attracts the hopeful of the world to its shores.

The Chinese Challenge

In discussing American exceptionalism it might be necessary to offer a brief critique on the challenge of the Chinese. This is important for two reasons. First, with the economic growth of China many have asserted the economic demise of America. The assumption is that within two decades China will surpass America as the leading economic power. Secondly, as a net debtor to the Chinese, many harbor the view that America has been diminished in the eyes of the world. In my view much of the optimistic talk about China becoming a world power supplanting the US has been exaggerated. There is no doubt that China has made tremendous strides over the last 20 years, but talk of American demise in the light of the aggressive growth in China's economy is overstated. America might be hurting at this time but there is no need for there to be the morbid fear of China that some people seem to have.

But America needs to get its house in order as far as China is concerned. It is estimated that China exports to America more than three times the goods and services than America does. This is neither free trade nor fair trade. The fact that China is a signatory to the World Trade Organization (WTO) makes little difference for China has been known not to play by the rules or to be too bothered by their enforcement. China simply wants to eat its cake and take it home at the same time and America over the years has allowed them to have a feast. The net result is that China has built up a massive surplus estimated in the region of about three trillion United States dollars largely on its trade imbalance with the rest of the world, America being the chief cornerstone of this imbalance.

The Chinese might be more surprised than any American that they have been allowed to get away with this for so long. Succeeding presidential candidates pledge on the campaign trail to deal with the "China problem" but as soon as they get into office such promises are forgotten. This has been the case ever since Nixon's rapprochement with China and China achieving Most Favored Nation status. This status has given China privileged access to the US marketplace despite its abysmal record on human rights which have only been met with tepid responses and unenforceable threats coming from successive US administrations. It is time that America asserts its own sovereignty and stand up to the Chinese instead of reacting when events occur that force it to respond.

What then is the fear? It is no secret that China is America's banker. This in itself would be laughable were it not for the serious implications of what this means for US sovereignty and its financial security. America is the cradle of capitalism and China remains the largest communist country in the world. It should be that America would have mastered the art of capitalism to the extent that it would be a net lender to the Chinese. But the reverse is true that today China is America's leading banker holding close to 7.5 percent of the nation's debt. With this level of indebtedness to the Chinese, it is not difficult to conclude that America ought to deal nicely with its chief banker since it may restrict the nation's ability to write checks. But even this assumption is overblown and is in fact too generous to the Chinese. This conclusion is arrived at for a number of reasons.

To begin with, talk of Chinese disinvestment in America is just that: talk. If China decides to call in its chips and begins a gradual disinvestment in America, where will it put its money? Saudi Arabia? An economically challenged Europe? Russia? The fact is that despite America's present weakness the Chinese know that America represents the best option for the investment of their sovereign funds. Despite America's foolish game of flirting with default on its debt, the country has never defaulted on its obligations. The global investment community instinctively knows there is no other place where its investments can be really safe than America. Despite the fluctuations of the American dollar on which the world's financial fortunes are pegged, it still remains the global currency of choice for commercial transactions. The truth is that China needs America more than America needs them. It stands to lose more than America does.

Furthermore, China also stands to lose more in a trade war with the US than the US does with them. Although China has four times the population of America, the country is heavily dependent on the US marketplace for its goods and services. Despite its large population, the Chinese marketplace is not robust and sophisticated enough to absorb China's output of goods and services. It will increasingly depend on the world market, especially the US market to do so. That they are capable of this output is already self-evident. The Chinese have a legendary work ethic which will stand them well into the future. It is this work ethic that has resulted in the considerable expansion of the Chinese middle class which means that more people are being lifted out of poverty.

In fact, the expanding Chinese middle class may yet prove to be a double edged sword that will create a nightmare for China's ruling elites. It is clear that Chinese economic liberalization has not been matched with political liberalization. Many analysts of the "Chinese miracle" are agreed that China will not be able to sustain its rapid economic growth and expansion without a serious shift towards political liberty. As more Chinese become members of the middle class, their thirst for political liberties will only increase. Perhaps a scintilla of evidence in this regard is the increase in the number of bloggers in China in recent years. Some estimates put the number of bloggers to be well over 200 million. How will the Communist Party restrain this exploding creativity? What will happen when the numbers reach 500 million which is not farfetched given the rapid rise of the Chinese middle class? Will the world witness more repression of nationalist and populist sentiment?

Writing in the *New York Times*, Thomas Friedman, easily one of the most seasoned and respected journalists in America, rightly observed that the "Beijing Consensus" of economic liberty without political liberty may have served the Chinese well but it will not get it to the next level.[9] He argued that one of the reasons for this is that today's knowledge industries are being built around social networks and these call for open collaboration, the freer exchange of ideas and the formation of "productive relationships" within companies and around the globe. If Friedman is correct, and it is difficult not to see the veracity of this point, then China in the near future will be faced with the inevitable challenge to manage change with little chaos and less repression.

How prepared is America and the rest of the world to deal with this ferment of creativity that is bound to become part of the social landscape in China? The Nobel Peace Prize committee has already fired the first salvo by giving the 2010 Peace prize to jailed Chinese activist Liu Xiaobo. This award is a clear registration of the world's impatience with China's abysmal human rights records. The country cannot indefinitely hope to eat its cake (rapid capitalist expansion) and take it home (repressed political liberties) at the same time. Something will have to give either in the creation a more open and equitable society or towards greater suppression of freedom and human rights.

The relationship between the United States and China has to be maintained on a pragmatic basis. It should be clear to Washington by now that China refuses to be "punished" for its human rights abuses. The imposition of sanctions that create barriers to trade is not helpful in the long run. Flexing military muscles is a non-starter given China's status as a nuclear power. Having been emboldened by its economic success, China will not bow to the demand of any world power for what it would term as meddling in its internal affairs. Sanctions, grand standing and big talk will not work. Washington's best bet is to work within the framework of economic openness and to nudge the Chinese to the inevitable social change which the expanding middle class will demand. This, incidentally, should have been its approach to the Cuban problem. For China, this will demand more trade and cultural exchanges, not less. But trade has to be conducted on a basis that is both fair and free and where China has to be urged to play by the rules. The Chinese must recognize that equitable trading arrangements are what the world demands today. There can be no compromise on this and the Chinese know it.

Despite all the rhetoric, some of it coming from the Chinese themselves, China has no interest in a weak or weakened America. The bald truth is that an economically weakened America does not increase the prospects of a prosperous China. If China can get away with the current imbalance in trade with both countries it will happily do so. They may not say so loudly but no country is more conscious than China that they need a strong America in order to remain competitive and strong themselves. This is why they will not refuse to finance US debt anytime soon. Why rock the boat when they are benefiting royally from the arrangement?

The ultimate challenge of the Chinese to America is that while Chinese capital is readily available, and as was stated above, will continue to be available, America has to come to the self-realization, sooner than later, that it cannot continue to live off the sweat, hard work and savings of the Chinese people. This is not language that resonates well with those who believe in an exceptional America, but not only is it fiscally imprudent to do so; it is a matter of self-respect and national security. National self-confidence and self-esteem should have already convinced the country of the inescapable reality of moving in fundamentally new directions, but there seems to be no great urgency to deal with the nation's crippling debt problem. Despite the posturing from conservatives that the national debt is unsustainable, many conservative politicians are not averse to increasing the national debt when it is expedient for them to do so as happened under the G.W. Bush Administration. There is not a Washington consensus that says enough is enough.

The bald truth is that America cannot go on spending as it does, giving tax breaks to the richest among us, or fighting wars and maintaining military janitorial services around the world on borrowed money. No American household could be properly run in this manner. Unlike government, no household has a monetary printing mill or credit cards without limit. Each has to live within its means or live in chaos. But the federal government is allowed to run an operation where money can be printed on endless reams of paper on the assumption that the country can absorb any monetary shock to the system. The Great Recession which still haunts us should have shocked the country to the realization that there have to be fundamental shifts in the way the country conducts its affairs. Petulant politics will shut down a government but bold leadership must assume responsibility for fiscal prudence.

Another challenge that America has to deal with from China is that country's robust diplomacy around the world. While American politicians demonize each other and indulge in political cannibalism of each other's ideas, the Chinese have smartly and deftly embarked on a bold policy of world courtship. China is actively investing in Africa, Latin America and the Caribbean region. Sitting on close to three trillion dollars of reserve currency, the Chinese have the economic muscle to do this. The sad truth is that America cannot embark on this kind of aggressive global investment anytime soon as it would be doing so on borrowed money and rising deficits and not on real income. The Chinese are doing so on real income and they are doing so smartly.

In Latin America and the Caribbean region, literally in America's backyard, the Chinese have stepped up their investments in infrastructure projects, largely in road building and repair and in the oil and gas industry. It recently lent the Jamaican government US $400 million for infrastructural support and is presently embarking on other multi-million dollar projects on the island. In Latin America Chinese investment is on the rise. Reuters News Agency reports that the Chinese oil firm CNOOC has purchased a stake in Argentina's Bridas Holdings, has substantially invested in Cuba's metal industry, the Chilean and Peruvian copper industry, gas and pipeline assets in Ecuador and Bolivia. They have lent $10 billion to Petrobas, the Brazilian giant state-owned oil company, and $16 billion in the Venezuelan oil industry which will guarantee it a supply of oil for years to come.[10]. The Chinese are directly involved themselves in some of these projects, especially the infrastructural ones.

The pace of Chinese investment in Africa has been even more frenetic. In 2006 their investment in the area reached 50 billion dollars. Through their Ex-Im Bank credit facilities loans to African countries have increased without the fanfare or strictures that follow World Bank or International Monetary Fund behavior in this regard. Chinese investment is conducted on a pragmatic basis with a clear understanding of non-interference in the domestic affairs of the countries in which they invest. To the chagrin of the West, they invest on the basis of "strict business" and are not too easily constrained by issues of human rights. They are, however, concerned about how money is spent and insist on strict oversight over projects which they fund.

This strict business pragmatism often stands in contrast to the American approach which is often characterized by a lack of strict oversight as to how money is spent on its international projects. Iraq and Afghanistan come readily to mind. The American taxpayer ought to be outraged at the colossal waste of financial and other resources that has occurred in these countries. There has been no careful accounting for the billions of dollars that have been wasted in the rebuilding efforts especially in Iraq. There is no secret that the Karzai administration is corrupt, yet billions of dollars have been poured into his country without any robust mechanism of accountability to restrain the corrupt or to at least ensure that the borrowed funds are spent wisely. Members of the Karzai government must be pinching themselves and asking why they have been allowed to get away with this level of corruption about which the American authorities should have knowledge. At the end of the day America will have very little to show for its

> *While generosity and compassion are worthy virtues of a great nation, they have to be tempered with prudence and fiscal responsibility.*

generosity and there is no firm indication that the countries that are being helped are in a mood to say "thank you." Perversely, it appears that American generosity is being rewarded by a resurgent Al Qaeda in Iraq which may lead to a permanently fractured and divided country, if present trends of tribal discontent pick up pace. What will become of Afghanistan after America vacates that territory is anyone's guess. America seems not to have learnt the lesson that while generosity and compassion are worthy virtues of a great nation, they have to be tempered with prudence and fiscal responsibility. The country cannot allow itself to be made a laughing stock as a result of its profligacy at home and a beady-eyed "generosity without accountability" abroad.

It would be naïve to assume that Chinese global investment is built on their benevolence, philanthropy or goodwill. The deployment of Chinese capital abroad is predicated on their geopolitical strategic interests. In the Caribbean, for example, a great deal of its involvement is tied to its "one China" policy which is intended to lure these island states away from Taiwan. It is being seen that Taiwan cannot match Chinese financial mettle in this area. The Chinese will not admit it readily, but it is clear what their objective is to counter American influence in the world and to emerge as a superpower that can challenge the supremacy of America globally. They are doing this not by any pretension to military power, but by a stealthy "economic diplomacy" which seems to be working.

There are signs that the State Department is mindful of China's intentions and particularly of its strategic influence in the Latin American region. On April 6, 2005, the Western Hemisphere subcommittee of the House International Relations Committee, held hearings on China's growing Latin American involvement. The conclusion was drawn that increasing Chinese interest and economic linkages pose a future threat to US influence and interests in Latin America. They see the Chinese as a challenge to US supremacy in the Western hemisphere; that they are building a Third World coalition of interests that may be inimical to America's interests and values.[11]

Despite this, America should not react to Chinese involvement with geopolitical hysteria. The influence of China in Latin America is exaggerated and there need be no fear that the region will move out of the American orbit anytime soon. Trading relations between America and Latin America are still very robust despite the hiccups in the relationship caused by regimes that are antagonistic to America such as Venezuela and Cuba. In 2004 US imports from Latin America amounted to $255 billion. Its direct investment in 2003 was $ 304 billion. The proximity of Latin America to the USA and the country's traditional ties with the region provide a good leverage against Chinese influence. Migration patterns from Latin America to the USA, for example, cannot be overlooked. This is why it is of critical importance that comprehensive immigration reform be accomplished. Whatever the perceived threats concerning China's influence in the region, America has to be smarter in its assessment and response and avoid knee-jerk reactions which can lead to larger problems.

America must continue to prod China towards being a more open society that embraces full freedom for its people and which upholds their right to self-determination. This is a critical American value which is non-negotiable. It is by being faithful to its own homespun values that America can counter the Chinese influence in the world. A larger percentage of the world will embrace America's values for an open and free society than they will ever do China's close and often oppressive denial of those values. People are not risking their lives and that of their families to live in China but they are doing so to get to America. As China is forced to change by the Chinese people themselves, there is the possibility that greater democratic freedoms will be embraced. One hopes that when that time comes, America would have gotten its house in order so that it can remain that beacon on the hill that all freedom loving people in the world can believe in.

What Future for the City on the Hill?

There can be no doubt that the bellicosity and intransigence in our politics today do not make America proud. If American exceptionalism is understood as America having a special place in the world and maintaining a sense of respectability among nations; the ability to be counted on to do the right thing particularly in a time of crisis; the special ways in which the country responds to the needs of the least among us in the recognition of the imperative of social justice, then it is not hard to see the work that has to be done to keep the country a shining city on the hill. The task is made harder by a recalcitrant politics. Such recalcitrance casts doubt on the ways in which the ordinary citizen through the democratic process can participate and believe that they are part of a special and deep experiment called America.

But there are serious issues to be faced not the least of which is the present dysfunctional character of the nation's politics. As a country just emerging from an international economic recession, there are still vulnerabilities to be overcome; there is still more to be done to nurse the country back to robust health. This health cannot be predicated solely on economic determinism but by a moral and spiritual imperative that the country seems to be losing a sense of. There is no doubt that there is something foundational that has shifted in the nation's culture and time will tell whether this will be for good or ill. What is without question is that the deep, existential questions of purpose and meaning persist and beckon the best nobility of spirit that the American people possess.

How the nation responds to this call to higher nobility is yet to be seen. It has to be a response to what Dr. Orlowski (mentioned at the top of this chapter) described as the need to eradicate the evil among us. It has to be a call to personal responsibility as each citizen recognizes his responsibility to self, to neighbor, to society, and if he is a believer, to God.

Despite the problems that the nation faces, and will continue to face in the future, no one should be in a hurry to write its obituary. It may be in decline in many respects, but America is an extremely malleable society. It is this malleability that has helped it to weather some of the gravest crises that it has confronted over the years- from the War of

Independence, to the Civil War, to the Great Depression, to the ravages of Katrina and the British Petroleum oil spill in the Gulf, to the collapse of the financial system in 2008. It is this malleability and the elasticity of the American Dream that will continue to sustain the country in the years ahead.

. . . .
Notes on Chapter Five

1. President Dwight D. Eisenhower: Farewell speech to the nation, January 17, 1961)

2. Ibid

3. Joseph Stiglitz: *The True Cost of the Iraq War: $3 Trillion and Beyond* -Op-ed piece in the **Washington Post**, September 5, 2010.

4. Michael Sheer, *On European Trip, President Tries to Set a New, Pragmatic Tone*, **The Washington Post**, April 5, 2009)

5. President Barak Obama- Address to the United Nations General Assembly, New York, September 24, 2013.

6. Ibid

7. Ibid

8. Op cit

9. Tom Friedman, *Going Long Liberty in China*, **New York Times** Op-Ed -October 16, 2010.

10. Carl Bagh :Timeline- *Chinese investments in Latin America*-**Reuters News Agency**, March 15, 2010.

11.Kerry Dumbaugh and Mark Sullivan: *China's Growing Interest in Latin America*-**Congressional Research Service** report-April 20, 2005-http://www.fas.org/sgp/crs/row/RS22119.pdf

ABOUT THE AUTHOR

The Rev. Dr. Raulston Nembhard is a priest at the St. Paul Community Church in Orlando, Florida. He has earned degrees from the University of the West Indies, Yale Divinity School, Stetson University and the Reformed Theological Seminary. He is also a trained Marriage, Couples and Family Therapist and is presently a Registered Intern in the State of Florida. He is also a trained family mediator. He is the author of four other books:

You and your Neighbor in a Broken World;
Muslim Rage and Christian Arrogance: A Time for Reason, Repentance and Dialogue;
Finding Peace in the Midst of Life's Storms;
Your Self-Esteem Guide to a Better Life

He has also authored an E-book:
Radical Obedience and Discipleship in the Theology of Dietrich Bonhoeffer.

....

For consultation and speaking engagements please contact Dr. Nembhard at: **stead6655@aol.com. Website: www.drraulston.com.**

www.ingramcontent.com/pod-product-compliance
Lightning Source LLC
Chambersburg PA
CBHW060858280326
41934CB00007B/1103